MEWS ITEMS

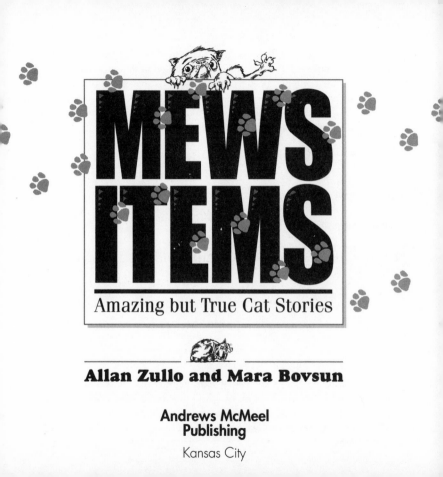

MEWS ITEMS

Amazing but True Cat Stories

Allan Zullo and Mara Bovsun

**Andrews McMeel
Publishing**

Kansas City

Book design by Pete Lippincott

05 06 07 08 09 BID 10 9 8 7 6 5 4 3 2 1

ISBN 0-7407-5042-9

Library of Congress Control Number: 2004111467

ATTENTION: SCHOOLS AND BUSINESSES

Andrews McMeel books are available at quantity discounts with bulk purchase for educational, business, or sales promotional use. For information, please write to: Special Sales Department, Andrews McMeel Publishing, 4520 Main Street, Kansas City, Missouri 64111.

To Bill and Gerry Kopack, who've been
purr-fectly wonderful friends,
and to Friskie and Kaya
for their years of feline friendship.

—A.Z.

To my sister Rhona, and our beautiful cats—
China, Kiran, Christa, and, most of all, Fuuss.

—M.B.

Contents

Cats Incredible!

CATS ARE AMERICA'S FAVORITE PETS. One out of every three households in the United States has at least one of the country's nearly 78 million owned felines. These cuties can be affectionate one moment and aloof the next; obedient at certain times and obstinate at other times. They are loyal, playful, and sweet—but only when they want to be.

They have been domesticated for 3,000 years, and we still haven't figured them out. But one thing we do know: Cats are fascinating creatures.

This book is a celebration of remarkable felines whose antics and adventures have astounded and amused their owners and admirers. In the following pages, you'll read a collection of amazing but true stories about:

- Unforgettable cats like the helmet-wearing Rastus, who rode thousands of miles perched on the handlebars of a motorcycle . . . Peaches, who nursed a baby squirrel . . . and Big Boy, who lived in a tree for three years and never came down.

- Feline survivors, including pets who endured the 9/11 terrorist attacks . . . an abandoned kitten found swimming miles from land in the Gulf of Mexico . . . and a cat buried under the rubble from an earthquake for nearly eighty days.

- Wacky cats who wound up in big trouble, such as the cat burglars who sneaked into neighbors' houses and

carted off clothes, shoes, and other personal items . . .
a "guard cat" who loved attacking mail carriers . . .
and a pair who liked to flush the toilet and flick on
the lights at all hours of the day and night.

- Traveling felines, including Skittles, who walked
  more than 400 miles in the dead of winter to be
  reunited with his owners . . . Tracker, who went for
  a nap under the hood of a car and wound up 150
  miles away . . . and Pip, who unwittingly got himself
  sealed inside a FedEx box and shipped hundreds
  of miles away.

- Courageous cats like Doc, who woke up his sleeping
  owners when their house caught on fire . . . Aggie,
  who drove an intruder out of her owners' home even
  though she was blind . . . and Reuben, who helped
  save two Chihuahuas during an attack by pit bulls.

Mews Items

From Abyssinians to Himalayans, from Persians to Siamese, from tabbies to calicos, the stories you are about to read prove that cats are simply incredible!

Feline Purrsonalities

HAPPINESS FOR RASTUS THE CAT was wearing a red bandanna and a tiny custom-made helmet and goggles while cruising the highways of New Zealand perched atop the gas tank of his master's motorcycle.

Rastus and his owner, Max Corkill, were the most unusual, if not famous, pair of animal advocates in the country. Together they traveled hundreds of thousands of miles, raising money for charity.

"Max used to have a little badge which said, 'cat chauffeur,'" recalled Adrian Brady, a member of New Zealand's

Society for the Prevention of Cruelty to Animals, a charity that benefited from the pair's celebrity status. "He used to chauffeur this animal all over the place—and the looks they got!"

It was quite a sight. With his whiskers blowing in the wind and his tail up, Rastus stood with his front paws on the handlebars of the classic 1952 Sunbeam S-7 Deluxe that his burly, bearded owner loved to ride. They always wore matching helmets and goggles.

The feline first met Max in 1989 when the black Bombay cross was just a kitten. Max, a motorcycle and car restorer, adopted him at a bike swap meet in Vancouver, British Columbia, after learning the cat had been abandoned.

A few weeks later, Max found Rastus asleep on one of the motorcycles in his shop. Even after Max started up the bike, Rastus didn't get off, so Max took the bike out and slowly picked up speed. The cat loved it, leaning forward with his front paws on the handlebars and back ones on the gas tank between the seat and the front tire.

From then on, Max would take Rastus on a daily ride and made a leather cover for the gas tank so the cat would be more comfortable. No matter what kind of motorcycle they rode, Rastus went along for the ride. Sometimes he would climb onto the front mudguard and enjoy the ride from that precarious spot.

In 1994 Max returned to his native New Zealand and, with Rastus, began raising funds for animal shelters and various other charities. They often visited schools where Max taught children the importance of caring for pets.

Every year Max and Rastus helped out on the Toy Run for Christmas, which was organized by a local bikers group who collected toys along the way for disadvantaged children. Max would be dressed as Santa while Rastus wore his imitation reindeer antlers and red bandana.

The biking duo soon attained such a following that they had their own fan club and starred in commercials for other products. Max started a company that sold Rastus T-shirts and other memorabilia with most of the profits going to the SPCA.

Rastus and Max had formed such a bond with each other that they even shared a joint checking account— Rastus's paw print was his signature.

"The cat was just like a person," said John Mahoney, CEO of New Zealand's Bell Tea Company, which used Max and Rastus in TV commercials. "Rastus used to come into the offices here and make himself at home. He would drink tea out of a cup [milk, no sugar] and would get quite testy when you took it away."

But on January 20, 1998, the duo's amazing road trip came to a devastating end. While riding on a BMW motorcycle, Max, fifty-eight, his girlfriend, Gaynor Martin, forty-eight, and Rastus were killed instantly when they were struck head-on by a car driving in the wrong lane.

As mourners—including more than 1,000 bikers—filled the chapel at the funeral of Max and Rastus, the hymn "All Things Bright and Beautiful" played in tribute to their remarkable friendship. The pair's matching helmets sat side-by-side on the coffin they shared. Max and Rastus were cremated together.

"Rastus was great, he was unique," recalled Adrian Brady. "This cat was a real bikie."

In a relationship that attracted worldwide attention and confounded naturalists, a stray cat formed a lasting bond with a hulking grizzly bear. They ate, played, and slept together.

The remarkable friendship developed at Wildlife Images Rehabilitation and Education Center, a twenty-four-acre facility near Grant's Pass, Oregon, that treats sick and injured animals. One of its occupants was a grizzly bear that had been orphaned as a cub in 1990, after being struck by a train in Montana. He sustained neurological damage and lost his sight in one eye. After his lengthy recovery, he was too accustomed to humans and too mentally impaired to go back to the wild, so he became a permanent resident at the center and was given the name Griz.

One July afternoon in 1995, Griz was served his normal meal—a bucket of vegetables, fruit, dog food, fish, and chicken. The 600-pound bear was lying down and eating with the bucket between his forepaws when a tiny orange kitten, no more than six weeks old, came out of the blackberry brambles inside the grizzly's pen. Looking thin and hungry, the little stray cautiously stepped closer to Griz, sat down, and meowed. Although Griz was a sweet-natured animal, he could be as violent as any bear when it came to food.

J. David Siddon, founder and director of Wildlife Images, watched in horror. "I was afraid that if I ran into the pen to try to rescue it, the kitten would panic and run straight for Griz," he later told reporters. "So I just stood back and watched, praying that it wouldn't get too close to the huge grizzly.

"But it did. The tiny kitten approached the enormous bear and let out a purr and a mew. I winced. With any normal bear, that cat would be dessert. Griz looked over at him. I cringed as I watched him raise his forepaw toward the cat and braced myself for the fatal blow. But Griz stuck his paw into his food pail, where he grabbed a piece of chicken out of the bucket and threw it toward the starving kitten. The little cat pounced on it and carried it quickly into the bushes to eat.

"I breathed a sigh of relief. That cat was one lucky animal. He'd approached the one bear of the sixteen we housed that would tolerate him—and the one in a million who'd share lunch."

A couple of days later, workers saw the kitten feeding with Griz again. This time, the feline purred and rubbed against the bear, and Griz reached down and gently picked him up by the scruff of his neck. After that, the friendship blossomed.

The feline—who the staffers named Cat—would curl up on the bear's chest or in the crook of his arm and nap with him. They played together like the best of friends. Cat would hide behind the pine trees in the bear's one-acre pen, then leap out and swat Griz's nose. The bear often carried Cat around in his mouth or let him ride around on his back. Sometimes Griz licked Cat until he was clean. Occasionally when Griz tried to pick up Cat by the scruff of his neck, he would grab Cat's whole head. But Cat didn't seem to mind.

"Their love for each other is so pure and simple," Siddon said in a 1996 interview. "It goes beyond size and species. Both animals have managed to successfully survive their rough beginnings. But even more than that, they each seem so happy to have found a friend."

The relationship was so strange that the odd couple was featured in magazines, newspapers, and television programs throughout the world.

The friendship lasted three years. But then in June 1998, Cat wandered out of the pen and never came back. Two months later, Griz died.

"We found Griz curled up asleep dead," staff member Barbara Rossman told the *Medford (OR) Mail Tribune*. "We don't know what he died of. But some of the volunteers here say it was of a broken heart."

When William Marcus's cat Baby disappeared, he assumed he would never see her again. Two years later, a filthy cat that looked just like Baby, only skinnier, appeared on his doorstep. Marcus wasn't sure if it was really his long-lost feline. There was only one way to find out. He told the cat to play pool.

The tortoiseshell cat had learned to play the game at the Nassau Billiard Rooms in New York, which Marcus owned. She was friendly with all the players who enjoyed seeing her knock balls into the pockets with her paws.

Sadly, she disappeared in 1921. "Maybe she was lured away by some rival who promised her daily fish heads and a life of ease," Marcus told the *New York Herald*.

But then on March 15, 1923, Marcus went to open up his place of business and was surprised to see huddled in the doorway a shivering, meowing cat that looked much like Baby, only this one was skinny, covered in dirt, and somewhat unsteady on her legs.

"I said, 'Baby, if that's you, where have you been for two years?'" Marcus recalled. The cat emitted a meek and plaintive meow. Not sure that she was Baby, but hoping she was, he put her to the test.

From a leather bottle he pulled out a pool pill—a "pea" with a number that corresponds with the number of one of the fifteen balls used in a billiard game called Kelly Pool. Marcus dropped the pill on the floor and the cat took a swipe at it and then sat down. Marcus was crestfallen. "It's not Baby," he announced to onlookers. If it had been Baby, he explained, the cat would have gently picked it up in her teeth, leaped onto the pool table, and dropped it into the leather bottle. "I had her for a year and she learned that all by herself," he said.

"Maybe it's Baby's daughter," he said. Then, in a hopeful voice, he added, "Maybe she's too hungry to do anything just yet." He warmed some milk, which the cat wolfed down along with two more bowls. Next, she got a bath. Now that she had a full belly, a clean coat, and new collar, Marcus gave her a different test—one that would definitely prove if she was indeed Baby.

After racking up fifteen balls, he called the cat onto the table and told her to have some fun. The feline pounced on the balls and, while lying on her side, began kicking them. With her first kick, she sent three balls into three different pockets. The second kick sent two more into a corner

pocket. With the precision of a hustler on a roll, she continued to kick or bat one ball after another into the pockets
until the table was cleared.

"Yep, it's Baby," her happy owner said. "Only cat in the
world that can do that."

Big Boy the cat was living the high life for years—in a tree.

Locals in Gulfport, Mississippi, claim that during
Hurricane Georges in 1998, the tabby was blown into a
sixty-foot oak tree in Jones Park from his home on the roof
of Lonnie Bobinger Sr.'s bait and tackle shop at Gulfport
Harbor. The cat remained in the tree for three years, choos-
ing not to come down no matter how wet, windy, or cold it
got. His decision to remain in the tree turned him into an

international celebrity. But then he disappeared—the victim of a catnapping.

Bobinger found the one-year-old cat in the tree after the storm, but he couldn't get him down. And no one else tried. Ron Roland, a retired mortgage banker, felt sorry for Big Boy, who got his name from his impressive girth, and began feeding him every day.

The cat ate and drank from containers that were nailed to a lower branch on the south side of the tree, and he wasn't shy about asking for seconds with a loud meow. He would let Roland and other pet lovers feed him by hand and pet him, but if anyone tried to hold him, he would take a swat. He used a branch on the north side of the tree for his bathroom. When he wasn't sleeping or sharpening his long, talonlike claws, Big Boy moved from limb to limb for exercise.

As word spread about Big Boy, children and local fishermen brought him treats. Then newspapers ran articles about him that were picked up by media around the world. The cat became a tree-mendous attraction. Some days, crowds of up to 100 people gathered, hoping to glimpse Gulfport's fat cat.

"People from all over send me food," Roland told the local newspaper, the *Gulfport (MS) Sun Herald*, in 2001. "A lady in Minnesota who heard about him sent me a check for $5.

"He comes from the school of hard knocks. He's not really like a cat. He's more like a survivor."

After three years of lazing around in the tree and being fed all sorts of goodies, the fat cat grew to an estimated twenty pounds. Roland was convinced the feline could have climbed down if he had wanted to, but he just loved being outside and letting others feed him.

Apparently, Big Boy descended from his perch at least once, though. "There was a bobtail cat who lived under the Coast Guard trailer," Roland recalled. "The bobtail cat decided to put his scent by the tree, and Big Boy came down and whipped [him]."

As his fame spread, Big Boy became the center of a local controversy. Some animal lovers complained that a tree was no place for a cat to live and they were upset by his bad diet and poor hygiene.

A veterinarian visited Big Boy in June 2001 and thought the cat looked healthy. "I didn't see any need for [rescue] at that particular time," Dr. Joe K. Brumfield told the *Sun Herald*.

But the day after the vet saw the cat, Big Boy disappeared.

An anonymous letter sent to local news media outlets claimed the cat had been rescued from "his unsanitary living conditions" and was being cared for in a loving home. And, oh, by the way, his name had been changed to George.

Roland, who worked at Gulfport Harbor Fuel and Bait shop, said he received an anonymous phone call from a couple who saw a woman with a ladder near the tree the day Big Boy was discovered missing. "He got catnapped," Roland told reporters. "I think she sedated him, to tell you the truth."

The catnapping triggered strong reactions among residents. For days Big Boy's fate was debated in the *Sun-Herald*'s Sound Off of the Day, a column in which readers could make comments anonymously. Among the remarks:

- "Of course they did the right thing. Why was Big Boy left there for so long? It's birds that belong in trees, not cats. I'm glad that there's some person in this state with common sense."

- "To the person who stole Big Boy: Who gave you liberty to take Big Boy from his home?"

- "If 'George' the cat was really catnapped for a life in a loving home instead of lonely misery in a tree, I want to say hooray, hooray to that compassionate person who rescued 'George.'"

- "I really don't think the catnappers did the right thing. He got used to living there [in the tree], and he probably won't be happy where he is. At least call him Big Boy."

Nothing more was heard about Big Boy until a year after the catnapping when this Sound Off comment appeared in the paper on July 16, 2002: "I want everyone to know about Big Boy. From the time he was taken from the park, he was loved and well cared for. He got sick and was taken to the vet and told that he had cat AIDS and cat leukemia and did not have long to live. So he was peacefully put down. That was much better than staying in the tree . . ."

A three-legged cat scaled a seven-foot wall and jumped onto a passing van in an apparent effort to find his deceased owner.

Ten-year-old Stowaway Jack was the beloved pet of Mary Carter, of Old Town, Wiltshire, England. Mary, a housekeeper at the Royston Hotel for nearly ten years, lived alone with the fluffy white feline, and the two formed an incredibly close bond. When the cat lost his rear right leg in a car accident in the summer of 2001, Mary took time off to nurse him back to health.

But then Stowaway Jack's world collapsed when Mary died unexpectedly in February 2002. The cat acted depressed and barely ate. Linda

King, Mary's daughter, was unable to care for him because she had two cats, including one that she claimed was "a bully and would have killed any cat with three legs," according to the local newspaper *This Is Wiltshire News*.

So Mary-Anne Phelps, manager of the Royston Hotel, agreed to care for Stowaway Jack and keep him at the hotel, hoping he would find comfort living in a place where his late owner worked. Everyone wished that the cat would enjoy the rest of his life there, happy and free among the guests and the serene setting of the courtyard. But the cat seemed restless, always prowling around the gated and walled grounds of the hotel as if he were searching for his former mistress.

Four days after he moved into the hotel, the cat took off. A guest spotted him taking an early morning stroll around the grounds. Suddenly Stowaway Jack scaled the gate and leaped over the perimeter wall. On landing, he jumped onto a passing van and has not been seen since, according to *This Is Wiltshire News*.

"I can't believe he managed to scale our tall walls," Mary-Anne told the paper. "Because he only has three legs, I'm very worried about him."

Mary's daughter was dismayed to learn that her mother's cat had taken off. But she understood why he did it. She told the paper, "Jack was probably pining for his owner and decided to go looking for her."

They never saw Stowaway Jack again.

Mews Items

A two-year-old cat named Blackie would have made the famed escape artist Houdini proud.

For about a month in 2003, the cat confounded workers at the Huron County Humane Society shelter in Norwalk, Ohio, by repeatedly breaking out of her locked cage and wandering around the office.

Perplexed shelter workers decided to see how she was escaping. They locked Blackie in her cage and stood around and watched. To their amazement, Blackie rolled on her back and dug at the corner of her cage, sticking out her front paw and lifting the latch from the outside. Then, with her back feet, she opened the top of the cage.

That wasn't the only door she opened, shelter attendant Karla Williams told the local newspaper, the *Norwalk (OH) Marion Star*. Blackie unlocked a door between a playroom and the front office by stretching from a chair to the flip handle. After shelter attendants moved the chair, Blackie simply jumped up and pulled the latch on her way down. Workers then duct-taped a doorstop to the floor so that Blackie couldn't open it, Williams said. They decided against locking the cage because they were afraid she would hurt herself.

In honor of her skills, the staff nicknamed the cat Houdini.

Eggbag the cat was one tricky kitty. For years, he astounded New Yorkers with his famous card trick.

One day in 1975, the gray-white cat walked into the Magic Center, a magic shop on Eighth Avenue, and stayed there, stealing the heart of owner and magician Russ Delmar. The cat was given the name Eggbag after the trick in which an egg is palmed out of a felt purse.

To earn his keep, Eggbag learned a card trick. He would lounge on the counter in the store while Delmar shuffled a deck of cards. "Pick a card," Delmar would tell a visitor, fanning the deck.

The visitor would select a card without showing it to Delmar or Eggbag and slip it back into the deck. The visitor then would straighten the deck before Delmar would fan the cards in front of the cat.

Eggbag would yawn and stretch. Then suddenly he would bite a card, pull it out of the deck with his teeth, and let it flutter down. The card would be the exact one that the visitor had selected. Every time.

"How does he do it?" said Delmar, repeating a visitor's question. "He does it very well."

Duffy MacNab was known as "the king of ship's cats."

As the mascot of the Scottish ocean liner *Caledonia*, the large black cat was always the first to land and the last to board. The feline had been with the Anchor Line's ship since its maiden voyage in 1905 and had traveled more than 300,000 miles back and forth across the Atlantic without missing a single trip.

Whenever the ship arrived in port, the cat would take off—often jumping from the deck to the roof of the pier— and not be seen again until it was time to sail. "Just before the gangplank was taken in, he would come marching aboard with all the dignity and self-importance of the king of cats that he was," the ship's physician, Dr. Mark Jenkins, said.

"He was an aristocrat through and through. He would only partake of the choicest food and was unusual in that he preferred tea to milk."

The sailors of the *Caledonia* always referred to the cat as "The MacNab." No one called him Duffy MacNab except the passengers who noticed that his full name was engraved on the metal collar that he wore.

Sadly, The MacNab's eightieth crossing proved to be his last sea trip. On August 3, 1913, the *Caledonia* arrived at the Anchor Line's pier in New York. Anxious to test his shore legs, the cat took a chance by attempting to jump from the forecastle to the roof of the pier, a distance of about ten feet. He had leaped from the deck to the roof on previous dockings, but only when the ship was much closer.

"The MacNab was in a hurry to get ashore, and so he threw caution aside and jumped," reported the *New York Times*. "His black body glistened in the sunlight, and then like a broken aeroplane, it began to drop. Rocket fashion, it fell through the air, and a moment later The MacNab struck the water. The sound of the splash was heard both on the pier and on the ship."

Seeing the cat's death leap, Quartermaster Angus MacLean immediately dived into the water and desperately searched for the mascot, but to no avail. "The grief-stricken MacLean was hauled back on board," said the article. "The sailors crowded him. There were tears in the eyes of some of them. They had all loved Duffy MacNab."

Purser Iain Johnson told the *Times*, "We shall never see his like again for he was indeed a rare cat. So loyal to the ship, and with it, all so intelligent. It is hard to lose him."

A ragtag cat named Minnie gained a reputation among sailors as the most licentious, itinerant feline ever to sail the seven seas.

She was either pregnant or getting pregnant on ships and docks from Singapore to Sydney, from Montevideo to Montreal, from the Caspian to the Caribbean.

Her infamy had a rather inglorious beginning when, in 1912, the crew of a British tramp loading coffee in Santos, Brazil, fished out a young cat that somehow had ended up in the harbor waters. The sailors gave her a bowl of milk from the galley and named her Minnie. She joined the crew for three successive trips to Canada.

She was never a cutie, but her appearance gradually worsened. Most of her once-fine tail was lost when it got caught in the gears of a winch at the Panamanian port of Balboa and one of her ears was chewed off during a dockside brawl with a dog in Prince Rupert, British Columbia. Because of catfights at various ports of call, even chunks of her fur were missing.

Minnie's reputation for catting around with every tom in every port grew with every pregnancy—and there were many. While her prolific pregnancies had become the ribald joke of the shipping world, her offspring reportedly were sailing on vessels to all four corners of the globe.

Kitty-making wasn't necessarily a good thing. In 1915, near Buenos Aires, Minnie presented the captain of the ship with a fine litter of Argentine kittens. The captain wasn't amused and banished her and her brood to a lumber schooner.

Eventually, Minnie made her way to Montreal's waterfront, which at the time was a notorious cosmopolitan rendezvous for seagoing felines. Cats from Antwerp, London, New York, Rio de Janeiro, Lisbon, and Casablanca would roam the docks, enjoying their shore leave with toms and mousers from other vessels.

After World War I, Minnie joined a freighter from Portland, Maine, that took her to ports along the Black Sea. When a year passed without a litter, it appeared that she had settled down and was now living a celibate life. But one night, after forty-eight straight hours on the bridge, the exhausted captain returned to his cabin only to find that Minnie had given birth to five kittens—on the captain's bunk. He never forgave her. Weeks later, at the port of Danzig, Poland, he left the kittens on the dock and gave Minnie to the captain of a Cardiff coal ship.

For the next two years, none of the stevedores in Montreal saw Minnie, and they assumed she was gone for good. But in the summer of 1922, she showed up once again, this time arriving on a freighter from Hamburg, Germany, with three children from her latest litter. However, she and her whole family had arrived in disgrace.

Weeks earlier, the ship had taken on 450 crates of live canaries in Hamburg. During the crossing, Minnie and her progeny spent much of their time in the No. 1 hold. They grew fat and happy. Near the end of the voyage, a ship's mate went down into the hold and counted canaries. The casualty list: 18 known dead; 147 missing.

Only the cook's pleas saved Minnie and her offspring from death by gunnysack in the briny deep. For the rest of the trip, the cats were kept in the grimy boiler room with the engineers. Although she was kicked off the vessel when it docked, it wasn't long before she had hitched a ride with another crew—who discovered, somewhere in the middle of the ocean, that Minnie was once again pregnant.

The motherly instinct of a ship's cat named Lady Maude was so strong that it cost the feline her life.

Lady Maude was the mascot of the crew of a freighter named the *Mary B. Hawkins*, which was carrying lumber from Tampa to New York in December 1912. In addition to the cat, Captain John Larkins kept on board many other animals, including a duck, chickens, horned toads, and a marmoset.

Early in the voyage, ten ducklings were hatched, but the mama duck wasn't acting very motherly—a situation that didn't escape the eyes of Lady Maude, according to a report given later by Captain Larkins. "A look of sorrow spread over the cat's features as the Lady Maude saw the indifference the mother duck displayed," said the captain, adding "she had different notions" about the way the ducklings were being brought up.

Late one afternoon, the cat took matters into her own paws. She chased the mother duck over the port rail, while the fowl quacked in protest. Because the cry of "duck overboard" wasn't considered important enough to turn the ship around, that was the last the crew saw of the mama.

Now that the ducklings were orphaned, Lady Maude decided to adopt them. "The cat at once addressed herself to her new occupation and in a few hours, the ducklings were following her as contented as though she were adorned in feathers and had webbed feet," the captain said. "The Lady Maude was gratified and even attempted to develop a waddle."

Sadly, the cat's life as the new mama came to a tragic end. On "wash day" aboard the ship, Lady Maude and her brood were perched at the edge of the forecastle hatch, watching the crew swab the deck below. The mess boy was filling a large tub of water by a railing when the ducklings, hearing the call of the wild, jumped down. "When the tub was filled, a series of infantile quacks was heard and the Lady Maude saw her adopted babies leap delightedly into the water," the captain said. "For a minute, I reckoned she was going in after them. She [was] resigned to watching them sink. But being ducks, they didn't sink."

Apparently, the Lady Maude didn't realize that. She jumped up onto the rail and tried to dive in after them. Unfortunately, she missed and went overboard. Unlike the ducklings, she couldn't swim.

Peaches loved to chase and taunt rodents, including squirrels, in the yard of her home in Manchester, New

Hampshire. So everyone who knew her was shocked when she became nuts over a baby squirrel—and began nursing her!

On April 19, 2002, Peaches, who was very pregnant, and her fellow feline Cream were lounging in the home of their owner, Mary Silveria, when a baby squirrel that had been nesting in the chimney fell down into the unlit wood stove. The infant squirrel lay there, frightened and confused.

Mary named the poor critter Kato and at first tried to keep it away from Peaches because of the cat's penchant for tormenting such little animals. But impending motherhood had caused a seismic change in the feline. Rather than chase Kato, Peaches adopted it. Mary and her family were amazed as Peaches picked up the baby squirrel and begin to nurse it. "I just couldn't believe it," Mary told the local newspaper, the *Manchester (NH) Union Leader*.

Two and a half hours later, Peaches gave birth to four kittens on Mary's bed. The new mother then placed the little squirrel with her kittens and nursed all five of them together. She let all the babes, including Kato, suckle for three days.

But the strange adoption didn't last. Mary heard a squirrel making a ruckus on the roof of her house and figured it was Kato's mom. So Mary gently took Kato away from Peaches and reunited the baby squirrel with his real mother. So while the mama squirrel tended to her baby, Peaches did the same with her little ones.

To the amazement of onlookers, the daughter of a mother cat acted as a midwife and assisted her during the birth of a new litter.

It happened in 1947 at the Rockland Country Club near Nyack, New York, where a pregnant three-year-old black cat named Minnie Sr. and her equally black daughter from a previous relationship, Minnie Jr., lived.

According to witnesses, the younger cat placed her forepaws on her mother and pressed rhythmically throughout the two hours it took Minnie Sr. to give birth to four healthy kittens. Not only that but after each of the kittens was born, Minnie Jr. gave them their first baths and severed the umbilical cord.

Bill Shea, caddie master at the club, was strolling by some shrubbery when he spotted the two Minnies and a kitten who had just been born. When he saw what Minnie Jr. was doing, he called over other staff members and guests of the club to watch.

"She [Minnie Jr.] had her two front paws on her mother's stomach and she was stroking her, and pressing down just like she was giving her artificial respiration," Shea told reporters. "Sometimes she would put one paw underneath her mother, and sometimes she would have both paws on her together.

"And every once in a while, she would stop and go over to Minnie Sr.'s head and lick her face, just like she was comforting her, and then they would meow at each other softly as if they were talking to each other. Then she would go back to stroking her with her paws."

Shea and the others watched as Minnie Jr. bit the umbilical cords when the kittens were born and then licked them clean.

Minnie Jr., who lost her own litter a few weeks earlier, helped her mother nurse the kittens and acted as a babysitter whenever Minnie Sr. took a break from her brood.

A mother cat with social aspirations for her offspring gave up her young kittens so they could have advantages that she was unable to give them.

In the early morning of August 2, 1931, a homeless New York cat took her newborn kittens in her mouth, carried them to the swank Central Park Zoo and dropped them inside the cage of Numa, an aristocratic lioness. Her maternal instincts aroused, Numa consoled the mewing infants and purred contentedly as the kittens nuzzled next to her for warmth.

Numa's purring was so loud that it caught the attention of zookeeper James Coyle. He was surprised to see the lioness taking care of the kitties. Fearing she might accidentally hurt them, he took the little ones away from Numa—much to her dismay. Coyle tried to find the mother but he never did.

The mother's sacrifice paid off because Coyle adopted the kittens and raised them in style, feeding them scraps left by the royalty of the Central Park Zoo.

A mama cat went to great heights to have her litter—high up in a tree.

Moments before giving birth on April 12, 2004, the cat climbed an old cottonwood tree in Billings, Montana, and delivered five healthy kittens in a crook forty feet from the ground. By the afternoon, the cat had not come down with her offspring.

Her worried owner called the veterinarian, who warned that if the tiny newborns were left to the elements, they might not survive the nighttime cold, and even if they did, the sightless babies would probably fall out of the tree once they became mobile. Desperate, the owner called all over Billings seeking help and advice.

Finally, as darkness approached, she called the fire department. "Generally we don't do animal rescues," Battalion Chief Tim Bergstrom told the *Billings (MT) Gazette*. "But it was getting dark, and the woman had tried everything else."

With the lives of the kittens at stake, firefighters talked it over and decided to answer the call. A ladder was maneuvered into the tree, and firefighters retrieved the five kittens, much to the delight of the family's children and their neighbors.

Mama cat was none too happy that anyone had dared touch her babies, but she got over it once the kittens were safely on the ground, Bergstrom told the newspaper. The kittens and their mother were whisked inside the warm house.

"It was a happy ending for everyone," he said.

In a perplexing case of opposites attracting, a house cat chose as his best friend . . . a mouse!

A cat named Huan used to chase and kill mice just like the two other felines in the home of Charanai Nanoontum, of Pichit, Thailand. But then one day in 1999, according to news reports, Huan found a baby mouse in a closet and thought it was, well, the cat's meow. Huan, whose name means "fat," and the mouse, whom Charanai named Jerry, became instant pals.

"When Huan found Jerry, I thought she would eat the mouse as usual, but she didn't," said Charanai. "Love took over."

After the friendship blossomed, the cat began protecting the mouse from other cats and dogs, said the owner. Jerry returned the favor by periodically cleaning the cat's paws. The two liked to play and sleep together, and were often seen lapping milk from the same bowl.

The strange relationship brought worldwide attention to the cat and mouse, from CNN to the syndicated TV show *Ripley's Believe It or Not*.

Charanai said her other cats were baffled by the pair's relationship.

A mother cat and a mother hen formed their own cooperative family. In the early 1900s, Martha Wandell of Staten Island owned a Maltese cat that had four kittens. The felines lived in a roomy chicken coop with a hen that had eight chicks. The hen, the cat, and all their offspring got along just fine.

The cat protected the chicks from invading rats at night. "Because the chicks tended to attract rats, the cat never went hungry and gained easy nutriment from the rodents, to the advantage of her four young," said Martha.

In the daytime, the cat accompanied the eight chicks and their mother on their daily walks. She acted as their family friend and guard. Learning from their mothers, the kittens and the chicks became best of pals.

When a dispute arose over the ownership of Pinky the cat, the feline provided testimony in court that made for an easy verdict.

New Yorkers John Bonner and Catherine Borrho, who lived in the same apartment building, both laid claim to Pinky. Unable to resolve the issue, they went to court on March 11, 1931, and explained the problem to Magistrate Michael Ford.

When he learned that the cat could wink on demand, the judge asked Bonner to make Pinky do the trick. Bonner ordered the feline to wink, but the cat refused.

Then it was Borrho's turn. "Wink at the judge, Pinky," she said to the cat.

Pinky looked at the magistrate and slowly closed one eye.

"It's your cat, Miss Borrho," the judge ruled.

Soxy the cat was crazy about power. He just couldn't stay away from electricity.

In March 1999, the eighteen-month-old tabby wandered into a substation in Hull, England, and received the shock of his nine lives—an 11,000-volt jolt.

Normally, that's enough to kill a human being, but the cat survived. He was left with burned paws, singed fur and whiskers, and paralyzed ears and a front leg. He would have been a fried feline if an engineer from Yorkshire Electricity hadn't spotted Soxy and managed to carry him clear of a 132,000-volt live terminal.

Workers nicknamed the cat Sparky. When his picture appeared in the newspaper, his owner recognized the missing cat and was reunited with Soxy. The cat became a celebrity in the area as a regular at animal welfare charity events.

But like a pyromaniac drawn to fire, Soxy just couldn't stay away from electricity. "There was just something that drew him to that substation," his owner, Steve Bateman, told the BBC. "But I thought he would have learned his lesson."

Apparently not. Six months after Soxy nearly died from his electrical encounter, Yorkshire Electricity workers found the cat's singed, lifeless body in the same substation.

"I'm totally devastated," Bateman said at the time. "I can't believe this has happened after all he went through last time. He was very loyal and affectionate and he loved all the attention he got. I've decided I owe the little fella that final bit of respect, and I'm going to bury him in his favorite spot in the garden."

Presumably away from any power lines.

Minnie the cat was on the payroll of a multinational corporation. Her job title was chief mouser, and her pay was $4.40 a month.

From 1933 to 1946, Minnie kept the central research department of the Standard Oil Development Company in Bayonne, New Jersey, free of rodents. Her monthly salary—which was carried on the books the same as all the human employees—covered her meals of salmon and milk.

Shortly after the cat was hired, a recurring monthly item charged to "Minnie" puzzled a staid auditor going over the books of the Bayonne plant. A subsequent investigation disclosed that Frank Hatch, head janitor of the Standard Inspection Laboratory, had created a special position for the tiger-striped feline of doubtful age and even more doubtful ancestry.

The auditor made a stink about a cat having a salary, but he backed down when the president of the Standard Oil

Company of New Jersey questioned Minnie's boss about what provisions had been made for her under the company's annuity plan and other employee benefits. Minnie became a celebrity and was the subject of articles and photos published across the country.

She ignored several feline letters of proposal, including one from a tomcat that said his only fault was laziness but that "you have a good job and I'm sure we could manage very nicely." Instead, Minnie found her own loves, and during her thirteen years as Standard Oil's chief mouser, she had more than 100 kittens, all of which were in great demand to be adopted.

When she died in September 1946, her job was given to her ten-month-old son, Timmie Esso, who received a slight hike in salary to $5 to cope with the rising cost of living.

A sleek black cat named Dolly Lee had a chance to live out her life in luxury but instead she choose her old neighborhood under the elevated train.

When she was a kitten in 1917, she was given to Mrs. M. L. Meyer, who owned a haberdashery and a flower shop next door on Sixth Avenue and Forty-fourth Street in New York. Dolly grew strong and developed into a mighty huntress, slipping into open windows of basements on the block and finding plenty of prey.

She became the darling of the neighborhood. During the day she sat in the sunshine on the windowsill of the flower shop as passersby stopped to pay homage by petting her and giving her a friendly "Hello, Kitty."

When it was naptime, Dolly Lee would drift off to sleep on her favorite blanket amid the delicate scents in the flower shop. In the evenings she would go on rat patrol while continuing to enjoy attention from the residents.

In the fall of 1928, Dolly Lee's life changed dramatically after Mrs. Meyer—who, like the cat, was getting old—closed the flower shop, sold the haberdashery store, and moved with her pet into a swank hotel offering more luxurious surroundings. For Dolly, it was worse than a prison.

"Dolly was positively hysterical," according to a *New York Times* profile of the cat. "She was sent to a hospital, as is the way with all well-treated nervous wrecks. She was given medicine . . . All to no avail. Dolly Lee missed her audience. She yearned for the bright lights of the roaring forties . . . In some mysterious way, the neighborhood learned its pet was dying of ennui. Rats and mice were on a rampage. Dolly must come back. A formal invitation was sent to Mrs. Meyer by the owner of the haberdashery."

Mrs. Meyer understood and, with some misgivings, sent Dolly Lee back to the only neighborhood that the cat had ever known. But shortly after her return, Dolly Lee vanished. Neighbors conducted a search without success until one of them, on a hunch, got a key to the empty, dark flower shop. He went inside but didn't see anything other than a slightly open window. He was about to close the door when he caught a pair of feline eyes staring at him from an open, unused icebox. It was Dolly Lee, proving that you can go home again.

Talk about a fat cat!

What might be the current fattest pet cat in the world, Katy, a five-year-old Siamese from the town of Asbest in the Ural Mountains, has weighed in at fifty pounds—slightly more than the average six-year-old boy.

"She doesn't really eat that much," owner Tamara Yapugova told the newspaper *Komsomolskaya Pravda* in

2003. "She has a couple of fish in the morning and about 200 grams [seven ounces] of meat in the evening. We give her vitamins . . . and we don't begrudge her milk mixed with sour cream. Dairy products are very good for her, after all."

Katy had a waist of twenty-seven inches—a half inch longer than her length. She achieved her enormous size partly because she was fed hormones to stop her from mating. *Komsomolskaya Pravda* noted that despite her young age, Katy had completely lost interest in the opposite sex, including her "ex-husband," the household's tomcat Kiska. Her only interest was food—especially frankfurters.

Katy's owners tried to get her recognized in the *Guinness Book of Records* as the fattest living cat in the world, an honor held by O. T. Reuters, a forty-one-pound feline from Minnesota. However, a spokesperson for *Guinness* said it had stopped listing records for fattest pets after concern

that some pet owners were doing harm to their animals
while attempting to set new weight records.

A German feline named Mikesch weighed forty-one
pounds—six times a normal cat's weight—and was so
obese that he couldn't take more than four steps without
getting exhausted.

"You can call it cruelty to animals," shelter veterinarian
Karin Bartell told the press in 2004 as the six-year-old fat
feline stared at photographers with a bored look. "It's a
problem for joints and the heart. The cat can't clean
himself because he's too fat. He walks three or four steps
and is completely exhausted because the heart no longer
works properly and the cat can't breathe normally
anymore."

Adult cats usually weigh between 7 and 1[...]
should eat no more than about 10 ounces of [...]
according to veterinarian guidelines. Howev[...]
owner was feeding him 4.4 pounds of minced meat a day, so
it's no wonder the cat turned into a furry blob.

Officials at the animal shelter in Berlin became aware
of Mikesch's condition after his owner, an elderly man, was
taken to a nursing home and could no longer care for the
cat.

Mikesch was put on a strict diet to reduce his size. But
he felt so lost without his meat-feeding owner that the cat
stopped eating altogether. A shelter worker took Mikesch
home with her for ten days to help get his appetite back.

cat in the United States has lived longer than Granpa
Rexs Allen, a hairless Sphinx cross. The feline lived for an
amazing thirty-four years and two months.

The cat was about six years old when he was adopted
from the Humane Society of Travis County (Texas) in
January 1970 by Jake Perry of Austin, whose hobby was
showing cats and caring for sick and abandoned ones.
Granpa had been brought to the shelter after being found
wandering near a busy intersection.

Knowing that the cat was somewhat rare, Perry put
up posters in the Austin area, trying to find the owner.
Months later, Perry received a call from a French
woman who told him, "You've got my cat Pierre." She
said that in December 1969 she had been visiting her
daughter in Austin when someone had left a screen
door unlocked, and Pierre had taken off. The woman
had gone back to France without her cat. After the

woman returned to Austin for another visit, someone
told her about the poster, so she called Perry and asked
to meet the cat.

When she saw the feline, she announced he really was
Pierre, her long-lost pet. The cat had papers that said he
was born in Paris, France, on February 1, 1964, to Pierre II,
a Devon rex, and Queen of France, a Sphinx. But since
Perry was such a cat lover and had registered the cat as a
household pet under the name Granpa Rexs Allen, the
woman agreed to let him keep the feline.

Perry eventually began showing Granpa, who charmed
judges so much that he earned the rank of supreme grand
master, the highest award given to cats that compete in the
International Cat Association's household pet division. By
appearing in cat shows and living way past his life
expectancy, Granpa became an international celebrity and
traveled all over the world.

According to *Cats & Kittens* magazine, Granpa always got a vanilla cake with tuna and broccoli for his birthday.

Perry told the magazine that Granpa loved to go shopping at PetsMart. "If you said, 'PetsMart' to him, he was on your shoulder ready to go. He went everywhere with me, even grocery shopping. He got a checkup every two weeks."

Perry said that the cat got smarter with age and could tell the difference in colors. He loved pink. "If you put a blue or yellow sweater on him, he would pull it off," Perry recalled. "Pink would stay on. Also, if he was sleeping and some of the other cats were playing and woke him up, well, even an hour later, he would come down and slap them, and he knew which one."

So what did Granpa eat that helped him live so long? Several years ago, Perry told the *Austin (TX) American-Statesman*, "Every morning he has Egg Beaters—cats get high cholesterol like we do—and chopped diet bacon. And broccoli or asparagus. With coffee. Folgers, that's his favorite. I set a jar of mayo and a jar of red jelly in front of him. Whatever he puts his paw on, that's what he has on his bacon and eggs. No salt, he's on a salt-free diet." In the evening, Granpa received regular cat food, said Perry, who credits Granpa's longevity to his love of broccoli and other vegetables.

In the last few years of his life, Granpa suffered from fluid buildup in his lungs. He died in his sleep on April 1, 1998, from pneumonia.

After a short ceremony in which the two dozen cats living in Perry's house filed past Granpa's lace-lined infant's casket, he was laid to rest in Perry's backyard cat cemetery. President Clinton sent a sympathy card, as did more than 400 other friends of Granpa's around the world.

The *Guinness Book of Records* officially recognized his long life, listing Granpa as the second-oldest cat ever certified. The first was Puss, owned by Mrs. T. Holway of Devon, England. Puss passed away on November, 29, 1939—one day after his thirty-sixth birthday.

Some of the literary world's most famous authors had cats for muses, or at least for companionship. Among the writers' notable felines:

- Atossa. This Persian cat was immortalized by nineteenth-century English poet Matthew Arnold. In his 1882 poem about a canary, Arnold recalls the way Atossa would sit for hours, immobile, beside the bird's cage, never attempting to attack it, but never giving up hope that one day he would capture it.

- Calvin. He was a Maltese cat who arrived one day at the home of Harriet Beecher Stowe, author of *Uncle Tom's Cabin*. Calvin frequently sat on Harriet's shoulder while she worked on her manuscripts.

- Catterina. This large tortoiseshell cat was Edgar Allan Poe's pet and the inspiration for his story "The Black Cat." When Poe's wife was dying of tuberculosis in the winter of 1846, the couple was destitute. A visitor found the stricken woman lying on a bed of straw wrapped in her husband's coat and Catterina on her chest to keep her warm.

- Chin and Chilla. They were raised from kittenhood by noted author Paul Gallico. When he moved to England, Gallico gave them to publisher David Smart, who lived in a majestic Chicago estate. There they got "the silken-basket and caviar-for-breakfast" treatment. Later, Gallico visited his former pets, but they offered no fond greeting. Instead, he wrote later, they "exchanged a glance of total consternation . . . and fled," fearing he had come to whisk them from their soft life and back to his rustic New Jersey farm where they had been treated like cats.

- D.C. The husband-and-wife writing team of Gordon and Mildred Gordon paid two dollars to adopt a black cat from a Los Angeles shelter and named him D.C. He proved so smart and clever that he inspired them to write the book *Undercover Cat*. It sold millions of copies and was adapted to the screen in the Disney hit *That Darn Cat*, starring D.C. himself. The couple became wealthy enough to give the stray–turned–screen star his own dining room and a personal secretary to answer fan mail.

- Foss. This striped tabby was owned by nineteenth-century author and artist Edward Lear. Edward was so devoted to Foss that when he decided to move to San Remo, Italy, he instructed his architect to design a replica of his old home in England so Foss would suffer a minimum of distress after the move. Lear's drawings of his tabby are well known, especially those that accompany his rhyme "The Owl and the Pussycat." When Foss died in 1887 he was honored with a full burial in a grave in Lear's garden.

- F. Puss. Tough-guy novelist Ernest Hemingway was a softy when it came to cats because he allowed more than sixty of them to roam his estate in Key West, Florida. But one cat, F. Puss, was special. In fact the feline was regarded so highly by the author that Hemingway left his infant son, Jack—nicknamed

Bumby—in the cat's care, unsupervised by humans. "F. Puss lay beside Bumby in the tall cage bed, and watched the door with his big yellow eyes, and would let no one come near him when we went out," Hemingway wrote in *A Moveable Feast*.

- Hinse. He was a tyrannical tomcat who belonged to Scottish novelist Sir Walter Scott. Hinse constantly terrorized Scott's huge dogs, especially at dinnertime. One day, Hinse pushed his luck too far and was killed by one of the canines.

- Master's Cat. When Charles Dickens's cat, Williamina, produced a litter in his study, Dickens allowed one little female to stay on. She became known as the Master's Cat. One night, Dickens was reading by candlelight when the flame unexpectedly went out. Dickens looked up and saw the cat staring at him. The author thought nothing of it, relit the candle, and continued reading. When the light started flickering again, Dickens looked up just in time to see a cat's paw snuffing out the flame. Dickens got the message, put down his book, and started petting the cat.

- Rumpel. This feline friend of nineteenth-century English author Robert Southey had the longest cat name in literary history. It was the Most Noble the Archduke Rumpelstizchen, Marquis Macbum, Earle Tomemange, Baron Raticide, Waowler, and Skaratchi. Friends called him Rumpel.

Seventeenth-century Italian composer Domenico Scarlatti credited his cat Pulcinella for the composition of one of his sonatas. Scarlatti was dozing in his armchair when he was awakened by the sound of his harpsichord. "My cat had started his musical stroll, and he was really picking out a melodic phrase," Scarlatti wrote. "I had a sheet of paper and transcribed his composition." It became known as "The Cat's Fugue."

In 1890, a cat figured prominently in the London debut performance of piano virtuoso Ignace Paderewski. As the pianist walked on the stage, he saw a cat sitting near the piano. Paderewski whispered, "Wish me luck." The cat then jumped onto his lap, and proceeded to purr in concert pitch as the pianist played. The performance was a great success, and in honor of the feline, Paderewski entertained guests backstage by playing Scarlatti's "Cat's Fugue."

Never-Say-Die Cats

PRECIOUS THE CAT survived twenty days without food amid the debris of Ground Zero following the 9/11 terrorist attack on the World Trade Center.

"It's unbelievable," her owner, D. J. Kerr, told the *New York Post*. "It's a miracle. I can't believe she's alive."

D. J. and her husband, Steve, lived in an apartment building across the street from the Twin Towers. The couple was out of town when the towers collapsed, blowing out the windows in their loft and filling it with flying glass, metal, dust, and smoke. A house sitter had been due to arrive that morning to take care of Precious, who had never been outside before. The Kerrs thought Precious had been killed because their seven-story building was severely damaged and unfit for occupancy.

But no one had counted on the nine-pound white Persian's will to live.

On October 1, 2001, emergency workers responded to a report of a cat crying on the roof of the apartment building. It was Precious. They used a recovery dog to corner the injured and terrified animal on the debris-cluttered rooftop. Then they brought her to the nearby Suffolk County SPCA van, which had been treating rescue and search dogs for exhaustion and exposure, according to the paper.

Suffolk SPCA chief Roy Gross called Precious's survival miraculous. "This is the first good story we've heard," he told the *Post*.

Precious managed to survive by drinking from puddles of contaminated rainwater, but they caused sores in her mouth. She was dirty and dehydrated. Her eyes were injured from the flying glass and she had lost two pounds. Her paws were burnt on the bottom because the roof of the building was so hot.

But when Precious was reunited with her owners, she began purring. She was especially happy when she was given her favorite food—sliced turkey. The cat made a full recovery.

Tweety-Pye, a five-year-old cat, showed incredible resourcefulness after her owner was forced to leave her behind in an apartment building that was evacuated following the 9/11 terrorist attack.

In the aftermath of the towers' destruction, animal advocates in New York mobilized quickly to remove pets trapped in evacuated apartments. The ASPCA began working with city authorities to let designated people pass through security barricades and go into apartments to rescue animals.

One of the pet owners aided by the ASPCA was Kathleen Ross, who had to leave her downtown apartment building without taking her beloved Tweety-Pye.

"I was going nuts," Kathleen told the *Christian Science Monitor*. "She was all I could think about."

Five days after the attack, a police officer who was alerted by the ASPCA managed to reach Tweety-Pye. He discovered that, unlike many pets, the clever cat was living quite well and looking perfectly healthy.

The yellow-eyed gray feline had managed to pry open the kitchen cabinet where her bag of dry cat food was kept. She dragged the bag into the living room, tore it open, and ate from it. She lapped up water that had been left in the sink.

Not only that, but she had found a way to stay comfortable. Probably frightened by the constant sirens and loud noises outside the building, she had pushed open a sliding closet door, nudged a pillow inside, and fashioned a safe nest for herself in a quiet corner.

"About 99.9 percent of the rescues had happy endings," Ruth First, a spokesperson for the ASPCA, told the *Christian Science Monitor*. The group brought more than 200 pets out of the empty buildings, and almost all were reunited with their owners. But none were as resourceful as Tweety-Pye.

A ten-week-old kitten was found dog-paddling furiously in the open waters of the Gulf of Mexico three miles from shore. Nobody knew how he got there.

He was rescued by a group of friends who were in their seventeen-foot boat looking for scallops off Homosassa Bay, Florida, on July 3, 2004. Their catch of the day turned into the cat of the day.

Zipping along the water at thirty-five miles an hour in their boat, the *Current Drift,* the fishermen spotted something bobbing in the water. They figured it was a plastic shopping bag, sea kelp, or maybe a sea turtle. As they got closer, they thought it was a dog.

Bob Burkenstock, who was operating the boat, turned the craft around to take a closer look. He, Bob Kline, and Kline's wife, Maggie Rogers, couldn't believe their eyes.

"There was a nine-inch-long kitten doing the paddle and screaming at the top of his lungs," Maggie told the *St. Petersburg (FL) Times.* "We scooped him up and he sat on the boat with me for eight hours."

For the rest of the day, Rogers held the cute, apricot-colored kitten in her lap, trying to comfort him while the others went scalloping. "He was exhausted and stressed," Maggie said. "His heart rate was high."

When anyone approached, he cowered and ran for cover behind Rogers's back. But he never cried. "I said to [her husband] Bob, 'Maybe he had screamed himself hoarse,'" Maggie recalled.

The boaters took the kitty back to a cabin where they were spending the holiday weekend and gave him a room of his own. He was terrified, especially of the sound of running water, and wouldn't eat or drink for two days.

When Maggie returned to their St. Petersburg home, the kitten took up residence in their shower stall—a dry one. The kitten was taken to Dr. Kevin Rose of the St. Pete Beach Veterinary Clinic. Aside from having worms, the ten-week-old kitten was in good health. He was adopted by Maggie's sister-in-law and given the name Nemo.

So how in the world did a kitten end up three miles out to sea? Was he an unwanted pet tossed overboard to die? Did he fall off someone's boat?

There were at least forty boats in the area. "He could have fallen off a sailboat," Wade Osborne, owner of Afishionado Guide Services, told the newspaper. Osborne, owner of three cats, added that if someone did throw the kitten overboard or use it as bait, "somebody that sick should be put on a hook himself."

A never-say-die cat was found alive in the rubble of a flattened house in Taiwan almost eighty days after the island country was rocked by a devastating earthquake.

The quake, which measured between 7.3 and 7.6 on the Richter scale, struck on September 21, 1999, killing 2,368 people, seriously injuring more than 10,000, and leaving more than 300,000 homeless.

Amid the tragedy, the Taiwanese received a few bits of unexpected positive news. Rescue workers found two survivors who had been trapped for five and a half days in their collapsed Taipei apartment building. Two dogs were rescued in Puli eighteen days after the quake.

But one of the most remarkable stories of all occurred on December 9—more than eleven weeks since the devastating tremor—when a brown tabby was discovered alive by workers who were preparing to demolish a damaged house. The feline, who was pinned down by furniture, was barely breathing and severely dehydrated. It weighed less than four pounds, half the weight of a healthy cat its size, and was comatose with a failing liver when it was found.

Apparently, the tabby had kept itself alive by eating another cat because a head, tail, bones, and bits of fur were found next to the survivor. It had lapped up rainwater that had seeped through the rubble.

A TV reporter who happened to be on the scene spotted the cat moments before workers would have thrown it in the rubbish. The reporter took the feline to a veterinary hospital in Taichung where it was placed in an incubator and fed via a syringe. Later reports indicated the cat recovered and was adopted.

The survival time for people trapped under collapsed buildings varies greatly according to the time of year, terrain, and any physical injuries. One theory says those who aren't rescued within forty-eight hours have a 10 percent chance of survival. The odds of a cat being found alive nearly eighty days later are incalculable.

A cat named Little One showed a lot of grit and determination after she was struck and maimed by a freight train.

Mike Hayes, of Sicamous, British Columbia, woke up on January 8, 2002, to find Little One lying next to him, bleeding and weak. She had lost a rear leg, her tail, and part of an ear. Hayes, who lived only a few hundred yards from the railway tracks, figured that a passing train had hit Little One. He confirmed his suspicion after following a trail of blood. "It threw her into the ditch," he told local television station CHBC. "Then she walked up and down the ditch and through the culvert and walked through the trees."

The injured cat eventually crawled up the ramp behind the camper that Hayes lived in, went through a hole in the roof, and waited for him to wake up. When he discovered the cat was seriously hurt, he rushed her to a veterinarian who put in eighty-three stitches to close her wounds. Within a week, Little One was becoming her curious old self again.

Hayes told the TV station that at one point he thought about putting his cat to sleep to end her suffering, but after seeing her make a remarkable recovery, he said he was glad he didn't. "You know you're loved when your cat comes home like that," he said. "She didn't give up on life. I won't give up on her."

Twinkles the cat took a tumble in a clothes dryer on high heat for fifteen minutes—and survived.

"It's a miracle he made it," his owner, Rachel Wallace, of Chippewa Falls, Wisconsin, told the *Chippewa (WI) Herald*. "This cat has now used up about eight and a half of his nine lives."

On April 8, 2001, Twinkles, who was adopted by the family in 1996, jumped into the clothes dryer when Rachel wasn't looking. Inside was a load of dry clothes that Rachel had put in the night before but had forgotten to take out. Moments after Twinkles leaped into the dryer unnoticed, Rachel decided to fluff up the clothes and closed the lid without looking.

"I put the dryer on high and went to sweep up in the kitchen," she told the newspaper. "About fifteen minutes later, I heard this huge clunking noise and went to check it out. It was horrifying." Twinkles was barely alive.

Rachel and her husband, Greg, brought the cat outside and poured cold water on him before rushing their cherished longhair to the vet.

"He was basically in shock," recalled Dr. Wayne Griffin. "It wasn't really dissimilar to an auto accident."

Considering that he was twirling around in a dryer that was heated to 160 degrees, it was amazing Twinkles survived. He suffered badly burned ears and a mangled tail, which had to be amputated. The cat also had fluid in his lungs caused by his exertion from constantly trying to right himself as the dryer spun.

For four days, the Wallaces used a syringe to feed liquid to Twinkles, who eventually made a full recovery. They credit the dry clothing in the dryer for saving the cat's life, because the pounding from wet clothes probably would have killed him.

Ever since the ordeal, Rachel said she always looks inside her washer and dryer before turning it on. But she didn't need to worry about Twinkles. He always stayed clear of the laundry room.

A one-year-old shorthair was the victim of either curiosity or a cruel prank on September 22, 1997, after it survived twirling in a washing machine for nearly half an hour. The stray was rescued at the end of the spin cycle by Marcella Coleman, a resident of an apartment complex in Elyria, Ohio.

Coleman took the cat, who was so dizzy he couldn't stand up, to the veterinarian. The feline was suffering from a concussion and chest and head injuries.

Coleman suspected that someone had put the cat in the wash. "I think it's terrible," she said in a CNN report. "As a matter of fact, I'd like to stick them in there and see how they feel about it."

The cat made a full recovery and was put up for adoption by the Elyria Animal Protective League.

A plucky cat that was trapped in a three-inch-wide space between two buildings miraculously survived for nearly two years before he was finally rescued.

The tabby belonged to the John Poppelaurer family, who lived on the top floor of a four-story apartment building in New York. On September 1, 1902, when he was still a kitten yet to be named, the feline fell off the roof and down into a crevice that separated the building from the one next door. The kitten survived the fall but couldn't get out of the confining gap, which had been bricked up on both sides. Every time he tried to climb up the bricks, he slipped and fell. So he yowled incessantly both day and night.

Residents tried to rescue the kitten by rigging poles together and putting them down to the bottom of the crevice in the hope that he would try to crawl up on them. Unfortunately, their efforts failed. Pieces of meat were

fastened to string, and lowered in an attempt to catch the
cat like a fish. But that didn't work either.

After a week, the neighbors became divided into two
camps—those who wanted to shoot or poison the cat to
put him out of his misery and those who believed that as
long as the feline was alive, there was hope for his rescue.
The cat lovers prevailed, and named the kitten Holey,
after the hole he had put himself in. Every day they
dropped food to him, and every night a woman lowered
a can of water for him.

Meanwhile, Holey continued to grow, but because of
the confining three-inch-wide space, his body remained
more or less squished.

News of the cat's predicament finally reached the SPCA.
"The agent who came to investigate was for killing the cat,"
reported the *New York Times*. "The women almost mobbed
him for his cruel point of view. He suggested shooting it,

but the cat's friends argued that he might thus jeopardize the safety of the occupants of the two houses. He tried the poison liver scheme but the cat, though excluded from contact with its fellow felines, had instinctive wisdom, [and didn't eat it]. The agent finally gave up."

On July 22, 1904, a cowboy who had been visiting New York heard about Holey and came to the rescue. An expert at handling the lariat, the cowboy went out onto the roof and lowered his rope. After a few tries, he lassoed Holey by the neck and then dragged the snarling, spitting, choking feline up to the top.

So what did the cat do after nearly twenty-three months of imprisonment? The moment Holey was freed from the rope and revived from the choking, he made a dash to get back into the chasm. Apparently, the cat was afraid of his suddenly spacious environment and of the humans who had kept him alive.

But Holey was caught before he had a chance to dive back down the hole. The cat—whose misshapen body looked like it had been squeezed in a vice (which, in a way, it had been)—was gently carried into the Poppelaurers' flat, where he nervously paced back and forth. It took several days before he calmed down. Eventually, he settled into a quiet life as a house cat, a very compressed house cat.

A black cat had the bad luck of being trapped for two months under a concrete floor of a building under construction.

The cat might never have survived had it not been for a surprise visit by health and safety inspectors. During an examination of the site in Newquay, Cornwall, England, on June 16, 2004, inspectors Steve Jones and Jonathan Harris heard faint meowing coming from under a block and beam concrete floor that had been laid back in April. Site manager Mark Tanner then instructed workers to break open a hole in the floor. When they did, a skinny black cat scampered out.

"It was certainly the worse for wear, but not actually harmed," Charles Gilby, another inspector, told the BBC.

After being given some water, which the cat eagerly lapped up, the feline was turned over to the Royal SPCA. At the shelter, an examination revealed he was underweight and dehydrated. He apparently had survived on droplets of moisture.

Animal collection officer Felicity Cross believed the cat, which was about ten years old, had been trying to escape. "His claws are really scuffed and broken, which suggests he's been scrabbling around trying to find a way out," she told the BBC.

Shelter workers gave the cat the name Houdini. "Generally, he was very subdued," Cross said. "He probably used up more than one of his nine lives."

A stray cat nicknamed Old Yellow stuck his head where he shouldn't have and wound up wearing a jagged piece of a glass fruit jar around his neck for several months.

No one knows for certain exactly what had happened, but at some point in November 2003 in Bryant, Arkansas, the cat put his head in an open jar and couldn't get it out.

Wanda Williams, volunteer director of the Animal Orphanage in nearby Benton, told the local newspaper, the *Benton (AK) Courier*, that she thought the cat had been after a rat. When the cat was unable to free himself, he broke the jar by banging it against something. Unfortunately, he was only partially successful. For several months, a portion of the jar remained around the cat's neck like a saw-toothed collar, forcing him to hold his head at an upward angle.

When animal lover Howard Johnson discovered Old Yellow's predicament, he tried to help, but the cat wouldn't let anyone get near him. So Johnson set out a trap, but the wily feline wouldn't take the bait. Instead, for months, Old Yellow managed to scavenge for food without cutting himself on his razor-sharp collar.

Finally in mid-February 2004, the cat was captured in the trap. Johnson took him to a local veterinary clinic, where the cat was anesthetized and freed from his misery. The jagged ring wasn't all that he lost. The cat was also neutered.

"It's hard to imagine how uncomfortable Old Yellow was during all those months, but now he's okay," Williams told the *Courier*. "And Howard is taking care of him again."

I shot an arrow into the air.
It fell to earth, I knew not where
But then I learned of news so sad
That I had struck a cat named Chad
(With apologies to Henry Wadsworth Longfellow)

A pet cat that was in the wrong place at the wrong time was skewered by an arrow that ran nearly the entire length of his body . . . and he lived.

On August 11, 2001, Chad went out the cat flap of his owners' house in West Bloomfield, Michigan, and wandered undetected into a thicket behind the yard of a neighbor who was shooting arrows at a target. In a stroke of incredibly bad luck, an errant arrow missed the target and struck Chad. The triple-blade tip entered above his tail and stopped just below his neck, narrowly missing his spine.

The archer was unaware that he had shot the cat, and Chad managed to head home where he crawled under the front deck and whined in pain. Hearing his cries, owners Milton and Mary Dolan pulled Chad out, who was then rushed to Union Lake Veterinary Hospital in nearby Waterford.

Administrator Annette Liendo told the *Detroit Free Press* that about twelve inches of arrow was removed, including the tip. "If you can imagine someone sticking a knife in your back, that's essentially what it's going to feel like," she said.

While Chad was recovering, the Dolans' daughter, Maribelle Mathews, went door-to-door to see if anyone

knew what had happened. When the archer heard
about Chad, he went to the police department,
said West Bloomfield Police captain Tim Sheridan.
The man was visibly distressed when he recognized
his arrow after officers showed it to him, the captain told the *Free Press*. The archer, who police
declined to name, said he had no idea his arrow
had hit the cat. He had looked for the arrow in the
brush, and wondered why he couldn't find it.

The Dolans' neighbor felt so badly about the
accident that he offered to pay all medical costs,
which topped $1,000.

Fortunately, the cat made a complete recovery
despite suffering the slings and arrow of out-
rageous misfortune (with apologies to William
Shakespeare).

A mother cat and her five kittens were trapped in a frozen snowbank and would have perished if it hadn't been for a persistent, nosy dog.

Mike Lalley and his yellow Labrador retriever Jessie were walking in open farmland behind their home in Cedarburg, Wisconsin, on a cold January day in 2001. Suddenly Jessie bounded off and then stopped in the middle of a field and began digging frantically. Lalley whistled repeatedly for her to return, but she refused.

After he walked over to his excited dog, who was still digging, Lalley saw fur protruding from the frozen snow. Thinking that Jessie had found a dead creature, Lalley nudged it with his toe. He was startled to see a cat raising her head.

Jessie's whimpers turned to barks. Lalley held his dog tightly as he bent down to examine the scene. He realized that the cat was trapped, her fur frozen to the hard-packed snow. He later told the *Milwaukee Journal Sentinel* that he chiseled the cat from the snow by pounding on the icy crust with his glove. One of the cat's paws was particularly difficult to break free, he said. "Basically, the fur around her body was frozen into the snow. She was stuck."

When he finally freed her, the bedraggled cat was too weak and sick to run away.

Looking into the hole of the snowbank, Lalley made an even bigger discovery. Five shivering kittens were inside huddled together. It was obvious that the grown cat had been on top of them, trying to keep them warm.

Figuring they were suffering from hypothermia, Lalley brought the cats to his home and began to warm them in the bathroom. At the same time, Jessie was desperate to make sure her little charges were safe. "She sniffed nonstop at the crack under the door," he said.

"I didn't think the cat that was on top was going to live. The others slept four or five hours, and then they were running around, kicking up a storm."

When morning came, Lalley brought his recovering feline family to the Ozaukee Humane Society, where the cats snuggled in blankets and heating pads and were given warm food. The humane society determined that the adult cat was the mother of the kittens, which were all less than a year old. Apparently, they were house pets who had been lost or abandoned.

"It's truly amazing that they lived," said Jennifer Pierce-Sylvester, executive director of the humane society. The animals were treated at the shelter for exposure and later put up for adoption.

For discovering the homeless feline family, Jessie was honored by the North Shore Animal League America, a Port Washington, New York, organization that gives out a monthly award to a deserving pet. Said league official Kristin von Kreisler, "This inspiring and unusual survival story tells of compassion shown by both dog and cat."

A kitten was found alive inside an ice chunk that had fallen from a car's wheel well.

Roberta Johnson, of Lake Crystal, Minnesota, spotted the large chunk on the street. Such pieces of ice are typical sights in Minnesota in the winter, but this one was different. She saw a feline face inside it.

"I was making a left-hand turn, the windows were down, and I went by this ice chunk," Johnson told local television station WCCO on January 9, 2001. "I noticed there was a little cat face in it. The first thing I thought was, 'Poor thing, it died.' Then I heard a meow."

She slammed on the brakes and saw that the kitten was trapped in the ice, and only its head was poking out. She broke open the chunk and freed the kitten.

Apart from having frostbitten ears, the cat was fine. Johnson kept the feline, and named it Car Cat.

When Nig the cat was being chased by a dog on a bridge that spans the river near Niagara Falls, she knew there was only one thing to do to save her life—she jumped.

The cat plunged 150 feet into the raging waters of the gorge.

Nig was the pet of customs and immigration officials at the American end of the long steel arch bridge. On April 6, 1922, witnesses saw a dog running after the cat and were shocked when the feline leaped off the bridge. The cat survived the fall and managed to paddle to the rocks at the base of an arch. Then she tried to climb up the steel beams, but it seemed futile. Efforts to rescue the cat were unsuccessful.

However, the next day, while officials pondered what to do, who should walk in . . . none other than Nig herself with ruffled wet fur, but no injuries.

When Tipper, a nine-month-old cat from Tampa, Florida, was in desperate need of emergency help, he did what we humans would do—he called 911.

On July 8, 1996, Tipper was home alone when he came within a whisker of losing one of his nine lives. "He got his flea collar stuck in his mouth and started choking," his owner Gail Curtis said. "He panicked and apparently was racing around the room."

Somehow, the frantic feline knocked the bedroom phone off the hook and, luckily, stepped on the speed-dial button that Gail had set to 911.

"I happened to be cruising in the neighborhood when dispatch told me they had received a 911 call and that no one was on the other line," Deputy Joe Bamford told the *Tampa Tribune.* "I rushed over to the house and broke in. That's when I found the cat gagging and going crazy. I found a handyman next door to help me. We grabbed the cat and wrapped Tipper in a towel, and, with the handyman's help, I removed the collar."

"I was so relieved that Tipper survived. Thank goodness he was smart enough—well, actually, lucky enough—to dial 911," his owner said.

A starving cat saved his life by telegraphing a message.

According to a news account on September 3, 1907, the cat was the pet of the employees of a Michigan branch office of an unnamed telegraph company. When a strike was called, workers closed the office and locked up, not realizing that their tabby had been left behind.

Days later, the chief telegraph operator at the main office in Detroit noticed an undecipherable message over the wire from that branch, which was supposed to be "dead." The dots and dashes were unintelligible, but he knew the office had been locked up. The operator thought a thief had broken in and was meddling with the keys, and promptly called the police.

"When a policeman got inside," said the news report, "he found the office cat upon the table, starved to a skeleton, working one of the keys with its paws—whether for companionship of the noise or through an instinct which told it that the man who formerly presided there had called to the outside world by that means."

It's not easy to kill a cat.

According to an account from the Canadian press on June 1, 1933, a man identified as I. Quick of Sault Sainte Marie, Ontario, owned a cat that appeared to have a broken leg. To end its suffering, Quick put the cat in a bag along with several rocks and tied it tight. He and some friends then went to the edge of Michipicoten Falls and he threw the bag in the water. They watched the bag slip over the edge of the falls and plunge 123 feet to the rapids below.

Quick and his buddies took their time getting back to his house. When they arrived, they were shocked. There, sitting on the front porch, was the cat—wet and seemingly OK.

In its October 3, 1949, issue, *Time* magazine reported that Henri Villette, a sixty-seven-year-old barrel maker from Alençon, France, stuck an unwanted kitten into a small mail bag and set out for the Sarthe River to drown it. However, the man slipped and fell on the riverbank and plunged into the water. Witnesses saw the kitten wiggle out of the bag and swim back to shore. Villette wasn't so lucky. He drowned.

Storm drains and cats don't mix.

A cat was stuck in a sealed storm drainpipe for sixteen days before she was freed.

On May 11, 2002, a curious kitty named Chloe was snooping around a construction site near her home in Blenheim, New Zealand. On that day workers were capping off the exposed ends of an underground seven-inch-diameter storm water pipe to prevent animals and debris from slipping into it during a heavy rain.

It was also on that day that Chloe disappeared. When she failed to return home, her owners, Lesley and Allan Butland, searched the neighborhood, put up posters, and called animal shelters and agencies to no avail.

They had no way of knowing that Chloe had been buried alive in a pipe three feet below the ground.

For sixteen days, the thirteen-year-old feline paced up and down the dark and slender tube and mewed her heart out for help. She was able to stay alive by lapping up droplets of water seeping through a gap in the cap of the pipe. Day after day, Chloe continued to meow . . . until finally someone heard her.

According to the *Marlborough Express* (New Zealand), when construction worker Michael Birtwistle arrived at the work site on May 27, he heard the cat's cries. Birtwistle and two workers uncapped the pipe and peered inside. They discovered a bedraggled and emaciated Chloe, who was so sick and weak that she couldn't move. The pads of her paws had become completely worn down from constant pacing. Half of her fur was gone, she had lost over half of her weight, and she appeared to be temporarily blind.

The rescuers had to use a piece of hooked wire to catch her collar and pull her limp body out of the pipe. The cat was rushed to a nearby veterinarian clinic where nurses were shocked to discover that her temperature was so low that it wouldn't even register on a thermometer. She was put on a heated intravenous drip and given doses of vitamins and minerals.

Because her owners had been so diligent in trying to find Chloe, the clinic was able to contact them right away. "She's in a pretty sorry state at the moment," Lesley Butland told the newspaper. "She was a big cat and she has lost half of her body weight. When they washed her, she looked like a rat. But now she squawks and you tickle her and she purrs, which is wonderful. She is a courageous wee cat."

On March 4, 2004, the Weymouth (Massachusetts) Fire Department received a call saying a cat had her head stuck in a storm drain grate. When the Engine 1 crew arrived, they found two-year-old Homer trying desperately to free her head from a two-inch-wide square hole in the grate, according to the *Weymouth (MA) News.*

Assisted by the Weymouth animal control officer, fire-fighters tried unsuccessfully to free the cat. So the rescuers removed the entire 250-pound steel grate, with Homer still stuck in it. The cat and her unwanted neckwear were carefully placed in the animal control officer's van and transported to the VCA animal hospital in South Weymouth.

Veterinarians sedated Homer, lubricated her fur, and slipped her head from the grate. After being held overnight, Homer was sent home—perhaps a little less curious about storm drains.

In April 1996, a stray cat found himself trapped for an estimated two weeks in a storm drain in Brookhaven, Long Island.

When Sheila Olszewski, a member of the Paumanok Cat Fanciers, learned of the feline's plight, she contacted town officials and received permission to uncover and access the entrance to the underground storm drain. A NYNEX work crew nearby agreed to help by opening the drain and providing the ladder, but it was up to her to find the cat. Olszewski descended thirteen feet into the storm drain. Once underground, she located a filthy, pathetic, scrawny cat perched on a ledge in the drain. Securing it to her chest, where it clung tightly, she climbed back up the ladder to daylight. The rescue happened just in time. On her way to the veterinarian, a heavy rain pounded the area and soon flooded the storm drain.

The vet concluded that the cat been down in the drain since a freak Easter snowstorm two weeks earlier. Fortunately, other than being frightened, dirty, and hungry, the cat was in fairly good shape. He was neutered, inoculated, and cleaned up.

Olszewski adopted the cream-colored feline and named him Thomas Nynex O'Malley (Thomas O'Malley for the hero of Disney's film *Aristocats*, and Nynex after the phone company). His nickname was Nine.

The cat gained weight and turned into a healthy, happy feline. Later that summer, Olszewski, who regularly participated in cat shows, began showing Nine. At the Nova Cat Fanciers show, Nine was the highest-scoring household pet in show and repeated this feat at the Empire State show—remarkable triumphs for a cat that a few months earlier had been trapped in an underground storm drain.

At home, Nine still liked to spend his days in the cool basement, as long as it wasn't too dark. Olszewski said he wouldn't stay down there if the lights were turned off.

A six-month-old stray had a hot time at the Peugeot plant in Ryton, England.

In March 1999, the cat wandered into the plant and, without anyone noticing, went to sleep in the body shell of a Peugeot 206 on the assembly line. Unfortunately for the cat, while he was sleeping, the shell went into the paint-baking oven at a temperature of 145 degrees Fahrenheit, according to the British Web site catsinfo.com.

The workers noticed the cat half an hour later when the shell emerged from the oven. The cat was hot but alive, so workers used a hose to cool him down. Fortunately, he survived, although his four paws pads were completely burned off and his fur was singed. Workers named him Talbot, after the van the company once manufactured.

A cat that had been abandoned on a storm-ravaged ship survived alone at sea for three weeks by catching and eating flying fish.

The feline was a mouser aboard the Norwegian sailing vessel *Birgette* when the ship was battered in a severe storm in the North Atlantic in February 1895. Towering waves toppled the foretopmast, smashed the bowsprit, and destroyed the rudder. All the sails had been ripped or blown away.

When the seas calmed down, the rudderless *Birgette* drifted aimlessly. On February 21, the crew abandoned ship and was taken aboard the Philadelphia-bound steamship *Snowflake.* For whatever reason, the cat was left behind.

Twenty days later, on March 12, crewmen aboard the steamer *Potomac,* which was three days out of London, spotted the disabled *Birgette* and sent a party of five sailors to board her. Not finding anyone, they were about to return to their ship when First Officer Dogbein looked up and discovered an emaciated cat peering over the edge of the crow's nest.

The officer wanted to reach the cat, but none of the rigging was still standing, and no one cared to climb the mast. "He was about to leave the cat to her fate, when a few gently whispered meows smote upon his ear and awakened memories of home," said a news dispatch dated March 24, 1895. "He decided to have the cat or never again board the *Potomac.* He called for volunteers to save its life."

They threw a line over the gaff—a spar that extended out from the mast—and one of the sailors was pulled up near the crow's nest, but the cat hissed and swiped at him and cowered out of his reach. When the sailor was lowered to the deck, he told the others what he had seen in the crow's nest.

"He said that the cat was surrounded with bones from fish that she had eaten," according to the dispatch. "Then the question arose as to how she had obtained fish up there. As they talked, they watched the cat, and saw it wave its tail frantically. A bright object shot through the air, the cat struck at it with its paw, and it dropped to the deck. Officer Dogbein picked it up and found that it was a flying fish. The officer and men were simply amazed at what they had seen and determined at all hazards to get the cat."

The line was thrown over the gaff again, and this time the sailor was able to grab hold of the cat. With a flying fish that she had just caught still in her mouth, the cat was brought safely to the deck. "It looked the men over, and, still holding the fish, went to the man who had thrown the line, rubbed against his leg, and purred its thanks," said the report. "It was a poor-looking specimen of a cat, but it was taken on board the *Potomac*."

The cat, who also survived by lapping up puddles of rain-water, became a loving mascot for her new crewmates. The dispatch said, "Capt. Leitch of the *Potomac* declares that the cat has been entered on the ship's articles as one of the crew, and nothing can get it from his possession."

A mother cat and her three kitchens were in a sticky situation. In a disgusting case of animal cruelty, the felines were covered with industrial-strength, toxic carpet glue and left for dead. But despite the gooey mess, they survived.

The owner of a carpet recycling center found the two-year-old mama cat and her two-week-old babies stuck to one another and to the floor inside his facility near Phoenix, Arizona, when he came to work on March 29, 2004. He had no idea who the cats belonged to or who had tried to harm them.

The felines were taken to the Arizona Humane Society where workers had to carefully shave the kittens to separate them. Then workers did their best to remove glue and carpet foam from the body of each of the orange tabbies. There was concern that the glue-dissolving solvent could kill the little ones, but workers had no choice but to try.

Melissa Gable of the humane society told local TV station KPHO, "One of the kittens' eyes was closed shut with the glue. Another one had its paw glued to its abdomen."

Gable said the mother was fully cooperative. "She was letting us pet her, and didn't try and bite or raise a fuss. She really had a great temperament, and it's hard to see a cat that is so sweet go through such torture—it's heartbreaking."

Police believe vandals broke into the place over the weekend and for fun spread industrial carpet glue on the floor using a broom. Apparently, at least one of these vandals intentionally placed the cat and her kittens in the glue.

A Phoenix police officer said, "It was pretty disgusting. It kind of makes your stomach turn because they're innocent animals. It was pretty sad."

Following an investigation, Phoenix police arrested a juvenile who faced felony animal-abuse charges.

Fortunately, mama and her kittens pulled through, and two months later were adopted by loving families.

A five-month-old kitten named Chutney suffered a near-fatal case of the flue when she fell fourteen stories down an abandoned shaft.

Little Chutney slipped out of the New York penthouse apartment of Craig Perkins on March 14, 1966. His fiancé, Judy Crockett, and her friend Linda Klink began a search for the gray tabby. When Klink opened the door to the roof, she saw Chutney perched on the edge of the ventilator flue. Startled, the cat slipped and fell down the shaft.

Hoping that the kitten might still be alive, Crockett called the police department and the ASPCA. Arriving in a blue animal ambulance, the ASPCA agent brought out his best piece of equipment—a thirty-foot stick with a loop on the end. That was useless, so the police

department's emergency service division was
summoned.

First, they lowered a lengthy rope down to the
bottom trying to determine if the kitten was alive, but
they couldn't tell. Nevertheless, they made a full-scale
rescue attempt through the basement. Using a drill,
electric saw, and an acetylene torch, sixteen policemen
worked for more than eight hours trying to reach the
kitten. When they drilled through to the flue's base,
the kitten wasn't there.

Thinking Chutney might have landed on a ledge
higher up, management received permission from a first-
floor tenant to drill a hole in the kitchen wall of his
expensively furnished apartment. But that effort also
failed to find the kitten. Finally they gave up and left.

But Owen Bodden, the building's superintendent, refused to quit. "The cops had started in the basement and didn't find anything, so I figured I'd look for her on the second floor," Bodden told the *Herald-Tribune*. "I went and tapped on the floor. Chutney tapped back."

Bodden then punched holes in the wall of another apartment with a chisel and maneuvered a mirror into the ventilator flue. His hunch paid off because he spotted the kitten. "It was easy from there," he recalled. "I just knocked in another hole and pulled her out. She was dirty but OK."

When a reporter mentioned to Judy Crockett that Chutney had stirred up such concern in a city often branded as heartless, she replied, "Well, yes. Cats are so precious, aren't they?"

A kitten who had been perched on a bridge support column for more than a day leaped 100 feet to the ground and landed with barely a scratch.

The Corpus Christi (Texas) Fire Department learned that a gray kitten was trapped on the support beam of the Harbor Bridge on August 12, 2001, but because it was late in the evening, firefighters waited until the following morning to attempt to rescue him.

The next day, two firefighters in the bucket of a ladder truck inched toward the kitten, who hadn't moved at all during the night. The young cat appeared relieved that they were trying to rescue him and he moved closer. But then, in his eagerness to get off his scary roost, he leaped toward them—and missed.

He fell roughly the equivalent of a ten-story building to the ground.

When the impatient feline missed the ladder truck bucket, firefighters watched helplessly. "It scared me," Fire Captain Lee Rogers told the *Corpus Christi (TX) Caller-Times.* "I covered my eyes. I didn't want to see it."

The kitten landed on his belly, spat out gravel, and was somewhat groggy at first. "It was an ugly sight, that's for sure," said Captain Joe Mihoin, who was in the bucket with firefighter Lionel Mendoza. "I thought it was toast."

And as improbable as it seemed to the firefighters who watched, the cat suffered hardly a scratch, although he was a bit dazed. The kitten, an eight-week-old domestic longhair, was taken to an animal clinic where an examination revealed that the only injury he had was a scraped nose.

It was the second time in a year that firefighters tried to rescue a cat from one of the bridge's support beams. Four months earlier, they successfully retrieved a black kitten who was trapped 150 feet off the ground. Fire department officials believe someone was abandoning cats at the bridge.

As for the leaping cat, "It's amazing because it fell almost 100 feet," Firefighter Rudy Davila told the *Caller-Times*. "Who knows how many lives it lost on the way down?"

The kitten ultimately landed in a new home. Davila adopted him for his three-year-old daughter, Katy, and named the cat Thud—after the sound the feline made when he hit the ground.

A gray tabby who was stuck on top of a thirty-foot utility pole in Canada for four days and three nights was finally rescued after officials agreed to turn off the power to the town.

On May 1, 2004, the cat climbed up a 25,000-volt power pole near Coalhurst, Alberta, south of Calgary, and wouldn't come down. After Calgary television CFCN aired a story about the "pole cat," several Coalhurst residents wanted to climb the pole to save it. But fire officials and the Royal Canadian Mounted Police stopped them because of the danger of the high-voltage lines.

The power company, Aquila Networks, was summoned to the scene by police to get the cat down. An Aquila lineman determined that approaching the cat would likely endanger it more. Typically when animals climb power poles they come down on their own after a time. The lineman said that if he were to approach the animal with large equipment, such as a bucket truck, the cat could get frightened and attempt to jump, endangering both the lineman and the animal.

After the TV station reported that the power company wouldn't attempt a rescue, hundreds of outraged cat lovers called Aquila in protest. Recognizing a public relations disaster in the making, Aquila relented. The company contacted Coalhurst officials to gain approval to cut off power to the town and surrounding area for a rescue attempt.

That evening, before a crowd of thirty onlookers, Aquila linemen de-energized a power line feeding more than 850 homes and businesses in Coalhurst. Then lineman Chris Donahue went up in a bucket and gently snatched the cat off the pole. Power was off for more than twenty minutes.

"The cat was pretty good till I went to reach for him," Donahue told CFCN. "He started to get a little antsy so I just took a hold of him and tried to be gentle and pull him off the pole and away we went."

Once on the ground, the cat scampered to shelter in a nearby yard.

No one knows how, but a stray kitten became trapped behind the dashboard of a car.

Theron and Diane Bryan, of Lakeland, Florida, heard a kitten meowing in their car, a Kia, on the evening of May 25, 2004. After searching around and under the vehicle, they pinpointed the source of the sound—behind the dashboard. However, they couldn't figure out how to reach the kitten because the space was so small.

The couple tried to coax the cat out, but that didn't work. Then the Bryans put two of their own cats in the car, thinking maybe they would lure the kitten to come out and play, but he wouldn't or couldn't budge.

Theron tried to take the dash apart, but he wasn't successful, so the couple took their car to the Michael Holley Kia dealership the next day. Five employees toiled for two hours before finally rescuing the gray kitten from the right side of the dashboard near the glove compartment.

Diane told the local paper, the *Lakeland (FL) Ledger*, that the kitten didn't belong to them, and she didn't know how he got trapped.

"Everyone heard it," Holley employee Elaine Rutherford said. "We were determined to get it out. We took everything apart."

The workers at the dealership didn't charge the Bryans for the cat rescue. It turned out to be a good deal for the cat as well. Rutherford decided to keep the kitten and named it Sephia, after the model of the Bryans' Kia.

A stray kitten wound up stuck in the front suspension of a minivan, and not even the fire department could free her. She was wedged in so tight that mechanics had to dismantle part of the vehicle to rescue her.

On December 3, 2003, Andrea Ventura, of Elk Grove, California, left her Aerostar minivan in a shopping center parking lot and went into a store. While she was shopping, she looked out and saw a kitten run up into the engine of her vehicle. Ventura went to her car and tried to reach the cat. It was futile, so she called the fire department.

Firefighters arrived and failed to entice the cat out. "It appears that the cat is caught up underneath the axle and the engine," Elk Grove Fire Department captain Jim Mackensen told KCRA-TV at the scene. "We've tried working our way through it for forty-five minutes . . . we're not going to get it out. We're going to have to dismantle part of the car."

The minivan was towed to the service department of Elk Grove Ford where mechanics discovered that the kitten had crawled up into an inaccessible place. As a result, the front end had to be taken apart. Three hours later, a very frightened and dirty kitten was pulled from the vehicle.

The rescue cost Ventura nothing but some anxious moments because the towing company and the Ford dealership donated their time and equipment. She adopted the cat and named her Aerostar.

Hell Cats

CAT BURGLARS HAVE BEEN PROWLING THE STREETS of big cities and small towns for years, and there's no end in sight. According to the delightful British Web site moggies.co.uk, which keeps track of such things ("moggies" is English slang for "cats"), there are among the more infamous prowlers so far in the twenty-first century:

- Tommy the tomcat, of Taunton, Somerset, England. He has been slipping out through the cat flap of his owner's home and returning with a booty of stolen goods. Among the items he's filched are shoes, designer clothes, a golf umbrella, and a bag of coins.

"It was funny at first," Tommy's owner, Ali Daffin, told the press, "but the haul just got more and more adventurous, with matching pairs of expensive [training shoes]. He would bring the left one home one morning and then two days later I would get the right. He hollers at the bottom of the stairs until I come down to inspect it all.

"I must have around fifty bits and pieces. It's becoming embarrassing. It looks like I've trained him."

- Midnight, of Simi Valley, California. In the dark of night, the marauding black feline has raided neighbors' homes, garages, sheds, and patios, stealing shoes, hats, shirts, socks, and even a wrapped Christmas present. Then he proudly carries them home to his distressed owners.

"We get so embarrassed by this," owner Sue Boyd told reporters. "We wake up in the morning and go out and there's stuff under the truck. The cat leaves things all over. We don't want these things."

"He's like a little klepto cat," her husband, Richard, admitted.

Each day, Midnight's owners leave a bag with the purloined goods hanging from their mailbox so neighbors can reclaim missing items.

The Boyds tried the most obvious option for Midnight's rehabilitation—locking him up at night. It didn't work.

For now, the Boyds continue to add to their daily collection of other people's stuff. "All we can do is laugh," said Boyd. "We feel sorry for the people who have to keep going out and buying socks and underwear. Somebody's definitely spending money."

- Holly, of Manurewa, New Zealand. This petite, friendly tabby has a shoe fetish rivaled by few others. She makes sure to get matching pairs and will determinedly retrace her steps to pick up the second shoe.

  According to published reports, neighbor Kay McKillion thought she was targeted by thieves when the seventh pair of shoes disappeared from her doorstep. She called the police to complain. "Every time someone walked past my house I would go out and see if they were wearing my shoes," she said.

  The mystery was solved when a neighbor told her about Holly. McKillion was directed to a nearby house where boxes of shoes lie waiting to be claimed.

  Holly's embarrassed owner, who asked the press to use only his first name, James, doesn't know what to do with his cat burglar, who collects three pairs of shoes in an average night's work. "She's not dangerous, she's not wild, she doesn't scratch," he said. "This is all she does."

But James believes that Holly knows she's up to no good, because she only steals when no one is looking.

- Dandelion, of Spotswood, New Jersey. The thieving cat first turned to a life of crime when he was a year old, and within two years he had stolen more than 700 items, according to his owner, Sara Peacock.

  "I own a cat burglar," she told reporters. "He goes into people's homes and steals things. It's an anxiety thing. He wants to please me by bringing me presents."

  The Oriental two-tone cat steals at least one thing a day. "His specialty is socks," Peacock said. "He'll bring home one and go back to get the other. We have lots of pairs but it's really embarrassing as it's not just one a day, it was up to five or six!"

Dandelion has expanded his collection to shoes, clothes, toys, purses, gloves, rags, pincushions, sun-hats, jewelry, and much more. The clothesline is no barrier to Dandelion because he has brought back clothes with clothespins still attached.

"Sometimes you see things dropped along the street and you know he's been collecting," said Peacock.

She used to go around the neighborhood trying to locate the owners of the stolen property but had little success. So now she leaves most things hanging on a tree outside the front of her house and keeps the valuable items inside. "I hear people walking past saying, 'Hey, that's mine.'"

Dandelion's curiosity got the better of him once when he sneaked into a neighbor's house and got locked inside for three days when they went away on vacation. "I had to call the police and get the window broken, which cost me $115," Peacock recalled.

She was so concerned about Dandelion's bad habit that she bought another cat to act as his playmate and occupy his time. But the plan backfired because Dandelion started collecting for his feline friend.

Other infamous cat burglars include:

- Moo. This seventeen-pound neutered male had a big-time jones for shoes. He roamed nightly through a five-square-block area of Guelph, Ontario, looking for footwear—shoes, clogs, work boots, even socks. "He goes nuts for socks, but only two rolled into a ball," his owner, Amber Queen, told reporters.

  If he couldn't find shoes, he would bring home other items, including magazines, toys, and gardening gloves. He had filched so many things that Amber put up a poster in the neighborhood that said, "Missing any shoes, gloves, etc? We have a cat burglar on the prowl." On the poster was Amber's phone number and a photo of Moo, unmasked as the shoe thief of Guelph.

Amber's mother, Susie, who lived with her, said she knew immediately whenever Moo had been plundering. "You hear a bang when he butts his head into the cat door," she told the press. "Then he maneuvers whatever he has inside. Then he goes out again. It gets so you hate to walk in the living room in the morning."

Moo's notoriety had grown so much that in 1999 the local newspaper, the *Guelph (ON) Mercury*, ran a daily tally of Moo's loot from the previous night.

- Major Benjie and Georgie. In the spring of 2001, this feline pair would sneak into the next-door neighbor's house and steal her cat's toys.

  Major Benjie, an Oriental tabby, started the crime wave by sneaking through the neighbor's cat flap and returning with a cuddly toy. Days later, the bold cat came home with more stolen goodies. Seeing how easy it was, his pal Georgie sneaked next door and returned with an expensive watch.

  Their little crime spree came to an end when their owner, Elaine Floodgate, of Charlton, England, spotted them going into the neighbor's house through the cat flap.

  "It all started when Major Benjie disappeared over the back fence and returned with a toy that wasn't his," she told the *Charlton Daily Express* (UK). "Then my neighbor mentioned her cats were losing their playthings."

Local vet Nick Adderley told the paper, "Georgie is the sort of cat you just want to pick up and cuddle, but he would probably lift your wallet."

- Minnimore. He was one of the first cats in England to gain notoriety as a klepto-kitty. He began his life of crime in 1990 when he stole a pink powderpuff from his neighbor's house. His owner, Cilla Karmel, of Tunbridge Wells, England, assumed it was an isolated incident. She was wrong.

  Over the next seven years, Minnimore sneaked into open windows and cat flaps of neighbors and snatched more than 160 items. Among the items were a fur hat, feather dusters, bedroom slippers, evening gloves, and, his favorite, stuffed animals, including three teddy bears from the room of a twelve-year-old neighbor. Karmel had to go around the neighborhood with a basket of stolen loot to find the owners.

Minnimore's avarice was boundless. "One night we heard this terrible banging," Karmel told reporters. "It was Minnimore, struggling to push an enormous jersey [sweater] three times his size through the flap."

The subject of many newspaper articles and stories on television, Minnimore was examined by a cat psychologist, who claimed that the feline was not really a criminal but merely acting out his need to hunt.

A house cat was so agitated over being locked in the kitchen that she unwittingly killed her owner.

According to China's official Xinhua News Agency, the cat's owner, identified only by the common Chinese surname Wang, had locked the feline in the kitchen of her apartment at night because the cat was in heat and making too much noise.

The report, dated February 25, 2004, said that the cat was trying to bite and scratch its way out of the kitchen when it accidentally ripped a hole in a gas cooking pipe. Gas leaked through to the bedroom of the apartment, located in the city of Shenyang. Wang died in her sleep from asphyxiation, but her daughter, who had been sleeping in the same room, survived and was recovering in the hospital.

The cat also survived by staying below the rising gas. However, the report said, the Wang family got rid of the feline, "and swore never to keep pets again."

It was double, double, oil, and trouble for Mandu the kitten.

The feline had wandered off from his home in Croydon, near London, England, and was snooping around a nearby building that was being demolished in 2004. During his exploration, the curious kitten fell into an old, open, partially full oil tank. Fortunately, he managed to climb out, but he was covered from head to paw with oil, and left a messy trail. Unfortunately for his owner, Robert Emmett, Mandu went straight home and into the house through the cat flap.

When Emmett returned home, he discovered that Mandu had left mucky paw marks everywhere, leaving him with an enormous cleanup bill of more than $1,000.

"When I walked in, the place was in such a state I thought we'd been burgled," Emmett told the news organization icSouthLondon. "It was everywhere, all over the carpets, the sofa, up the stairs, and on the beds. The smell was terrible."

Emmett said his insurance wouldn't cover it because the oil stains were classified as pet damage. His son Ben had to stay next door because of the oil fumes, although they had the windows open, trying to clear the house of the smell.

Meanwhile, Emmett rushed Mandu to the veterinarian because the cat became ill. "The vet thought Mandu had swallowed some oil when he fell in and then some more when he tried to lick himself clean," he recalled.

Mandu recovered and returned home with the family, who hoped he would never attempt another oil bath.

A cat named Bat terrorized postal carriers so much that they refused to deliver mail to his owner's house.

The carriers claimed they were afraid of the six-year-old ginger tom because he would rake their hands bloody when they shoved the mail through the cat flap. Not only that, but whenever he was outside, he would claw their legs with vicious swipes. The carriers used the cat flap because the house didn't have a mailbox.

In the spring of 2004, Bat's owner, Dan Coyne of Cranbrook, Kent, England, received a letter from the Royal Mail informing him that deliveries to his house had been suspended because of his "guard cat."

The letter, which Coyne shared with the *Sun* (London), said in part: "The postmen are experiencing problems with your Guard Cat. Sounds ridiculous, I know, but as they deliver through the flap, the cat scratches them. More incredible than this, your cat has been known to jump on the postmen's leg and dig its claws in."

Coyne told the newspaper, "I can't believe they are scared of him." But then he admitted, "Bat is a bit of a psycho and has been known to launch himself at people. He gets very wound up by the postman and sits under the cat flap waiting for him. As the postie pushes the letters through, I've seen Bat try to swipe him with his claws."

When the London press latched onto the story, the Royal Mail issued a statement claiming it wasn't funny. "The safety of our people is paramount, and attacks by animals are not amusing when you're at the receiving end."

Coyne had to collect his own mail at the post office until he put up a mailbox by the front gate of his house and kept Bat inside. In an understatement, Coyne said, "Bat does get a little stroppy"—British slang for belligerent.

Blossom was a sweet house cat who loved it when visitors would hold her and pet her. But woe to the person who would tease her, because only then would she turn into a vicious tiger.

The big gray cat was most fond of her mistress and enjoyed the comforts of living in a mansion in Boston. One day, a young man came for a weeklong visit and soon discovered that Blossom was less a kind kitty and more a ferocious feline. According to an article in the *Boston Transcript*, dated April 14, 1895, and headlined "The Strange Tale of a Resentful Cat," here is what happened after the man arrived at the mansion:

> He was an inveterate tease. As there was no one else for a victim, he took Blossom in hand, in spite of protestations. Her ears were greeted with strange terms, "Old rascal," "Scapegrace," "Tramp," and kindred names, till the astounded cat did not know what had come to her.
>
> Her pretty ways disappeared, she fled from his approach, and hid whenever she could till he was out of the house. One morning, she was missing for some

hours, and was not to be found in any of her hiding places. A loud cry from the chambermaid revealed her whereabouts. Blossom had revenged herself on the visitor's nightshirt, which lay in tatters on the floor.

Pussy was scolded, and everyone was cautioned to keep the [visitor's bedroom] door shut. In vain! The cat would find her way in and hide till the chambermaid was through for the day, and then the claws went to work, first on the visitor's own clothes and then on the pillow cases. The young man tried to soothe her feelings, but she would have none of him, and he was glad to cut short his visit.

Blossom quickly recovered her usual demeanor, and has never been known to destroy anything [since].

Bozo the cat committed murder in front of a dozen witnesses. But the merciless killer managed to elude the cops.

The feline fiend had been the well-behaved pet of the owner of the Long Island Bird Store in Brooklyn. Even though Bozo was surrounded by birds, he had never caused any trouble until the fateful night of July 16, 1948, when he turned into a bloodthirsty assassin.

The brown Angora was always let out after the store closed, but on the evening of the slayings he sneaked back in undetected while the owner was locking up. With the place to himself, Bozo turned from a sweet cat that tolerated birds into a stalking feline craving for fowl.

For his prey, he selected ten canaries flitting about in a wire cage that had been delivered to the store earlier in the day and placed in a big display window. As Bozo tried to break into the top of the cage, a growing number of passersby stopped and tried to find ways to prevent the looming massacre.

They pounded on the window. When that didn't work, they ignited rolled-up newspapers and waved them in front of the window to distract the cat. It seemed to work because Bozo abandoned the cage, only to attack another one containing several parrots. But he had a taste for canaries, so he soon returned to the first cage.

As he systematically punched through the wire mesh, the crowd yelled at him to stop. One bystander made an emergency call to the ASPCA, but because the shop was private property, the agency had no authority to break into the store.

Meanwhile, a passing patrol car stopped to investigate why a dozen people were swarming in front of the pet store. When police discovered that the cat was bent on canary carnage, they managed to contact the shop owner.

But by the time the owner opened the store, the cat had broken through the cage and consumed four canaries. Before police could arrest him on the fowl mass murder, Bozo slipped out an open door and fled into the night, leaving behind a trail of feathers.

Angus the cat, a firehouse mascot for years, ignited a blaze
of controversy over accusations that he had turned into a
horrible feline who displayed terrible hygiene and a disposi-
tion to match.

The ginger tom lived at the Birkenhead fire station
in Merseyside, England, ever since he was rescued from a
fire in 1986. He had been a well-liked, happy fire cat who
even had his own firefighter ID card. But in the summer
of 2002, a crew from one of the firehouse's four shifts
demanded that Angus be kicked out because he was urinating all over the station, had fallen asleep on the
kitchen's chopping board, and had become ill-tempered
in his old age.

One firefighter said, "It's got to be said that Angus is a
horrible cat. He's taken a chunk out of a few legs over the
years and now he's forgetting his toilet training. He's left
the odd damp patch on the chairs."

Firefighter Roy Stewart, who was leading the fight to oust Angus, told reporters, "He's got to go. This station has had thousands of pounds invested in it to make it a community fire station, where members of the public can come and look at the engines and see what we do. If any children come into contact with his mess, then that would be serious. It's time for him to be looked after somewhere else. It has been nice having Angus around for so long but we've got to face the facts. He's getting on and we can't look after him properly."

The anti-Angus faction wanted the cat put to sleep.

But crews from the three other shifts united in a "Save Angus" campaign. Pro-Angus supporters even had T-shirts printed up. "He's part of the furniture and we don't like the thought of getting rid of him," said a firefighter.

Firefighter Mick Loughlin, who first brought Angus to the fire station, said, "He's a very independent cat and we should leave him be."

The controversy caught the attention of the international press, and letters of support for the cat began arriving from around the world. "Everywhere we go now people stop us to give Angus their support," Loughlin said at the time. "We also have had letters from France, Germany and other places. Everybody seems to have rallied round him."

The *Liverpool Echo* asked its readers what they thought should happen to Angus: "Is he a bad-tempered old fleabag who deserves a dishonorable discharge from Birkenhead fire station? Or is he a loveable hero who should be allowed to live out his days among the friends he has made in sixteen years service as a lucky mascot?"

Echo readers voted overwhelmingly to save Angus. Of the more than 3,000 people who took part in the special poll, 82 percent said he should be allowed to stay at the fire station.

After weeks of bickering, members of all four shifts held a meeting and reached a compromise. Angus could stay. They agreed that a member from each shift would take on "Angus duties." A spokesperson for the Merseyside Fire Service said, "It was accepted that the firefighters who wanted Angus out did have a legitimate complaint and that the cat was perhaps not being looked after as well as he could have been."

With the cat-astrophe averted, Angus remained at the station for another year. But old age and deteriorating health forced him to retire in May 2003. He was turned over to a local cat lover to live out his life.

A spokesperson for the fire service said, "Angus has been a long-standing and loyal servant to the fire station and we've been very happy to have him, but as all fire-fighters have to retire, so does Angus." The firefighters—

even those who didn't much like him—bade him a fond
furwell.

A lobster-loving cat turned a popular restaurant into chaos.

Mattie was a friendly tabby who was adopted by
workers at Fay's Restaurant in New York. She was a good
cat and never caused any trouble, staying outside until
the last patrons had left and then eating delicious table
scraps later.

She was a fixture out front during the dinner hour. A
glass tank, where live lobsters were exhibited, was situated
on the sidewalk by the entrance to the restaurant. Mattie
enjoyed sitting by the tank, watching the crustaceans slug-
gishly move about. When a waiter got an order for a lobster,

he would take several out of the tank and the let the diner select one. Then the waiter would return the others.

On the evening of May 22, 1910, Mattie was so fascinated by the lobsters that she hadn't noticed Rose Leland, the restaurant owner's friend, arrive with her pet brindle bulldog Gus. While Rose sat down to dinner, the well-behaved dog was allowed to eat his own meal behind the hostess's desk near the front.

Mattie was watching the lobsters when a waiter picked out three, but one of them fell on the sidewalk. In a flash, Mattie jumped on it, but the lobster clamped one of its pincers firmly on the cat's tail. Filled with terror and pain, Mattie shot through the restaurant's open door, yowling all the way, the lobster still attached to her tail.

Although Gus was a trained, obedient dog, he was still a dog, and his canine instincts kicked in when he saw a cat running through the restaurant. He gave chase. Now Mattie had even more reason to be terrified. With the lobster refusing to let go, the cat dashed under and around tables with the barking bulldog in hot pursuit followed by waiters and Rose, who was yelling at the top of her lungs for Gus to stop.

Meanwhile, patrons were screaming, leaping up from their chairs, and knocking over tables. Plates of food crashed to the floor, silverware flew through the air, and tipped-over drinks splashed the diners' fine clothes.

Finally, the waiters captured Gus and Mattie and pried the lobster off the cat's tail. Gus was ordered to sit behind the hostess's desk, where he sulked. Mattie was locked up in the storeroom so she could recover from her trauma in darkened silence. As for the lobster, it ended up boiled and on the plate of a diner.

Gremlin was an alarming cat, and a clever one too.

The twenty-pound calico was one of three felines owned by Glenn and Nancy Erardi, of North Andover, Massachusetts. He and the other cats were fed their breakfast at around 3 a.m. when Nancy got up to go to work.

"Nancy isn't a morning person," Glenn recalled in an article he wrote in 1997 for *Cats* magazine. "She often hits the snooze button for an extra ten minutes of sleep, while the cats wait patiently near their bowls for breakfast to be served."

Gremlin, who displayed a take-charge personality, had a healthy appetite, and wasn't too pleased to be waiting around for his meal.

One morning, the alarm beeped shortly after Nancy had hit the snooze alarm, so, with her eyes half closed she fed the cats, showered, and shuffled into the kitchen for her first cup of coffee. When she glanced at the kitchen clock, it said 1:30 a.m. She figured it was really about 3:30. She checked the time on another clock, and it also read 1:30.

Assuming she had dreamed that the alarm went off, Nancy put the cats out and came back to bed. When the alarm sounded two hours earlier the next morning, she asked Glenn to check the clock. He couldn't find anything wrong with it.

On the third morning, the alarm beeped early again, this time shortly after midnight. The couple was perplexed. The cats seemed delighted.

"On the fourth morning the mystery was solved," Glenn recalled. "As Nancy reached to hit the off button, her hand landed on the back of Gremlin. Our mischievous kitty was advancing the clock by dancing on top of it—just so Nancy would feed her."

A cat stretched the patience of the United States Department of Justice.

In 1910, Speaker of the House Joseph Cannon (R-Ill.) lived next door to the offices of the Justice Department in Washington. He owned a large tomcat who was allowed to roam inside government buildings.

The feline loved to hop onto the desks of personnel at the Justice Department and satisfy his insatiable appetite for rubber bands. One of the clerks told reporters that the cat ate twenty-three rubber bands in one day and then, for dessert, devoured a pencil eraser.

"In consequence of existing conditions, the suggestion has been made that Attorney General Wickersham sue out a writ of injunction against the Speaker's butler, enjoining him from permitting the cat to jump the fence and visit the Department of Justice," said an account in the *New York Times* on May 14, 1910.

"Clerks in the department are willing to make affidavit to the animal's capacity for consuming rubber bands, which at the present high price of rubber, the officials say, is something to be considered."

A roving band of cockeyed, tipsy felines high on catnip turned a New York police station into chaos.

On the evening of September 12, 1904, Joe Weiss was sprinkling catnip on the pavement and attracting a large number of felines. A growing group of onlookers watched with amusement as the crocked cats wobbled and yowled along Fifth Street and Avenue B.

"Weiss, having collected a goodly number of cats, who came to the catnip from every gutter, roof, and basement in the vicinity like rats to the pipes of the Piper of Hamelin, started to lead his feline army along the avenue toward Houston Street," said an account in the *New York Times*. "Although Weiss walked steadily, the cats staggered like the Bowery after midnight, and emitted a maudlin caterwauling that led a few temperance advocates—and they were very few—in the crowd to protest to Officer Levy that it was a shame to lead the poor cats from the path of abstinence. They said that Weiss ought to be arrested."

The officer agreed and arrested Weiss on the charge of intent to intoxicate. But as he took Weiss toward the police station in Union Market, the cats followed them. "They weren't going to desert the good fellow who had brought them their lovely jag," the article said.

After Weiss was locked up in jail, the cats infested the place. They were in the cells, in the hallways, and in the booking room, "wailing Bacchanalian chants." A trusty chased them off the roof with a mop while officers scoured the station for stoned cats. Finally the trusty pulled out a hose and quickly sobered up the plastered pussies. "The Grand Feline Army of Weiss then dispersed into the gray remorseful dawn," the account said.

Later that morning, Weiss faced Magistrate Ommen, who, after learning what had taken place during the night, said, "This is the most extraordinary thing I ever heard of."

Weiss told the judge that he had used the catnip to see if he could hypnotize the cats and didn't mean for them to cause so much trouble. The judge reprimanded him and fined him $5.

The patrons of New York's Ansonia Hotel were convinced the ghost of a stray cat was haunting the building. For more than a week, spooky yowling had caused sleepless nights and frightened bellboys so much that they threatened to quit their jobs.

Those in the know believed the haunting was caused by a recently deceased black cat named Thomas who was seeking revenge.

One February evening in 1903, days before the eerie cries began, a stray cat suddenly appeared outside the sixteenth-floor apartment of Mr. and Mrs. John Edward Smith. When Mrs. Smith heard the cat meowing, she took him in and fed him a bowl of milk. Although the rules of the hotel forbid patrons from having pets, Mrs. Smith decided to keep him and made a bed for him in a drawer of her dresser. She named him Thomas.

All was well until Louis Jallade, the architect of the Ansonia, who also lived on the sixteenth floor, discovered that Mrs. Smith was harboring an illegal cat. "He did not tell Manager Webb about it, but decided to take the law in his own hands, excusing the assumption of authority by the observation that Mrs. Smith's conscience surely would suffer if she were permitted to break the house rules indefinitely," according to an account in the *New York Times*.

Without the Smiths' knowledge, Jallade kidnapped the cat and then summoned bellboy Thomas Gill to his apartment at midnight. When Gill departed Jallade's apartment, he was seen carrying a box under his arm. "This he carried to Eighty-first Street and Riverside Drive, where it slid accidentally from his arms and rolled down a high embankment to the New York Central Railroad tracks," said the *Times* article. "Gill says he thinks he heard a plaintive meow as the box descended."

Jallade and Gill assumed that this was the last they would see of Thomas the cat. However, a few nights later, the walls of the Ansonia began to echo with weird yowling noises. After Gill and Jallade confessed to some hotel staffers what they had done to Thomas the cat, word spread that the feline had been killed and was seeking his revenge by haunting the hotel.

Night after night, the creepy yowling rattled guests. Complaints came from the tenth floor up to the sixteenth floor. The disturbing noises were emanating from spaces between the interior walls that housed electric wires and ventilation conduits. Frightened hotel workers were ordered to search the building thoroughly but no one told them what to do if they spotted a spectral feline.

Just after dinnertime on March 3, when the orchestra had finished playing on the balcony overlooking the first-floor dining room, all the musicians had left except for their leader, Theodore Gordon. As he was placing his violin in its case, he felt a clawing at his leg. He looked down and saw Thomas, lean and emaciated. Suddenly, the cat jumped up onto Gordon's back and began pulling out tufts of hair from the top of his head.

"Screaming with fright, the musician bolted down the stairs ten steps at a time and landed like a catapult against the office clerk's desk," said the *Times*. "Thomas [hid] under a safe in the corner, and a dozen guests jumped after him. Eluding them, he ran up one flight of stairs after another, his pursuers hot after him. On the fourth floor, he jumped into an opening leading to the ventilated shaft.

"Ten minutes later, the office received a hurry call from Architect Jallade. Thomas had reached the ceiling of the sixteenth floor. With the pursuers looking on, a carpenter cut a hole in the beautiful wall of the architect's front room, and a bowl of fine cream was placed on a coil of pipes inside the shaft. Then a wire noose was fixed over the bowl, and it was not long before hungry Thomas had put his head into the trap."

After the cat was caught, Jallade wanted the police to take it away and destroy it. However, hotel staffers, relieved that the building wasn't haunted after all, begged officials to spare Thomas's life. He was allowed to sleep in a basket in the cellar before he was taken away to a new home—far from the Ansonia Hotel.

Two roguish cats learned on their own to repeatedly flush the toilet for fun, much to the chagrin of their startled owners.

One day in 2001, Russ and Sandy Asbury were alone in their home in Whitewater, Wisconsin, when they heard a toilet flush.

"My eyes got as big as saucers," Russ told the Associated Press. "At first, I didn't know if we had ghosts or what. I couldn't even imagine who or what was flushing the toilet."

Sandy went to investigate. She looked in the bathroom and saw her eighteen-month-old cat Boots standing on the edge of the toilet with his paw on the handle. The couple thought it was a fluke at first, until Boots did it again and again. Then their other cat, Bandit, also an eighteen-month-old, learned to flush on his own—or was taught by Boots.

"We have to shut the bathroom door when we go to bed," said Russ. "Otherwise, one or the other of the cats is in there flushing away all night."

The cats even started flushing while someone was using the toilet, he added. And they've both become skilled at unrolling the toilet paper and turning the bathroom light on and off.

"I've had cats all of my life," Russ said. "But these cats are different than any of the others." He added that the couple's water and sewer bills were getting so high that "the cats are going to have to get a job."

171

Barry and Nina Mortimer, of Essex, England, were flabbergasted when they received a phone bill in July 2001 for $414, especially since they averaged about $90 a month in calls. When the couple inspected the statement, they noticed a four-hour phone call to a $1.35-a-minute betting hotline, which offered tips and live commentary on horse races.

The Mortimers don't bet. But apparently their cat Persia wanted to play the horses.

Nina finally figured out that Persia had tipped over the receiver and pressed the preset button on the phone. She told the *Sun* (London) newspaper,

"I remembered coming down one morning and seeing the handset off the hook and hearing a voice saying, 'Your next meeting is at . . .' before I replaced the receiver. Standing next to the phone was Persia. She loves to walk over the phone to her favorite spot on the window ledge.

"The number was already programmed in when we bought the phone. We have settled the bill but will take steps to make sure this doesn't happen again."

Barry said, "From now on, it will be economy cat food for Persia."

Ryan and Annette Hale had to reprogram their telephone because their cats twice used the speed dial to call the police.

It was embarrassing enough in December 2000, when the Hutchinson, Kansas, couple's cat, Jasper James, stepped on their bedside telephone's speaker button and then hit the speed dial button that had been preset to dial 911. Naturally, the police showed up. Based on the meowing the emergency dispatcher had heard, the cops solved the identity of the caller.

But it became downright mortifying for the Hales when it happened again nine months later, on August 14, 2001. Only this time the culprit was their other cat, a three-year-old Himalayan named Kadie, who called the emergency number from the same bedroom phone. And it happened in the middle of the night.

Because of Kadie's call, the Hales were awakened at 3:30 a.m. by a police officer's loud pounding on the front door.

"We didn't know anything was going on," Annette told the Associated Press. "We heard this big bang at the door. My husband and I looked out the window and we saw it was the police. It was kind of scary, actually. I thought at first someone had died in the family, or maybe a wreck, a fire, or someone broke into our garage."

When Ryan went to the door and learned there'd been a 911 call from his house, he told the officer a cat was probably to blame. "He [the officer] seemed okay about it," Annette said. "Not mad or anything."

Annette, who reprogramed the bedside phone, admitted that the cat calls were embarrassing. But she added, "We think it's pretty funny. Nothing we can do about it now except laugh."

Pussy-Footing Felines

WHEN SKITTLES THE CAT MISSED HIS RIDE back home, he decided to walk. He trekked about 415 miles of rough terrain in the dead of winter over two states while avoiding wild animals and speeding cars for 133 days.

Charmin Sampson and her son Jason, sixteen, of Kelly Lake, Minnesota, worked at a water park in Wisconsin Dells, Wisconsin, over the summer of 2001. They lived in a trailer nearby with Skittles and their other cats, who often spent part of their days in the nearby woods. But when it came time to go home on Labor Day, Skittles was missing. Since school started the next day, the Sampsons reluctantly had to leave him behind. "We called him and called him," Jason told the *Hibbing (MN) Daily Tribune*. "We just couldn't find him."

But then more than four months later, on January 14, 2002, the two-year-old orange tabby showed up at the Sampsons' home in northeastern Minnesota. Jason opened the front door to find a bedraggled, emaciated cat slumped on the porch. At first, Jason couldn't believe the dingy cat with calloused paws and protruding ribs was really Skittles. But the feline was a neutered male that matched Skittles's coloring flawlessly. "I knew it was Skittles," he told Duluth TV station WDIO. "The cat is orange, with white paws and he's got a look to him—a unique look."

Incredulous, Jason carried him into the house where the weary feline ate some food and collapsed into a deep sleep.

"Usually when you bring in a stray, the other cats get to hissing and fighting because this is their territory," Charmin told WDIO. "Nobody was doing that. They were all kind of looking at him from a distance, checking him out while he was eating. And he was famished."

Within two weeks, Skittles had settled into his old routine, playing with the family's other cats and reclaiming his favorite spot on the living room armchair.

To this day, no one knows how Skittles made it home. "They [the cats] all went down [to Wisconsin Dells] in the back of the pickup truck," Charmin told the *Daily Tribune*. "They were all in their cages and they all had blankets over the cages, so they couldn't see out of the truck. I don't know how he would have known which way was home."

Skittles returned the day after Charmin's birthday. "It was a great present," she said. "I must be a good pet owner if he was willing to come all that way."

Grateful for his return, the Sampson family still is amazed by Skittles's long-distance trek. "I've heard stories like this before, but never believed them," Jason said. "Well, I believe them now."

Jello hated cars but loved his owner. During a car trip, the cat escaped at a rest stop and then walked ninety-five miles over five months to get back home.

In June 2003, Greg White, of Hesperus, Colorado, headed to the state of Washington to build a house, and took his cat with him. Knowing how Jello hated riding in a car, White had given his pet a sedative to keep him calm during the trip. But after about two hours, the cat woke up, freaked out, and started yowling wildly and scratching his owner.

Pulling off the road, White finally let the cat out of the car in a park in Monticello, Utah. Jello sat in the grass and calmed down for a while, but he became furious when White tried to put him back in the car and took off.

"I realized I had to say good-bye to Jello so I could continue my trip, which I did," White told the *Durango (CO) Herald*. After working on the house in Washington for ten weeks, he headed back home in August. On his return, he stopped off in Monticello, went into the library, which was located next to the park where he last saw Jello, and asked the librarians if they had spotted his cat. They all said no. He was resigned that he would never see Jello again.

But then in November, White returned to Hesperus from a brief trip to find a note on his door from neighbors who claimed they saw Jello in the neighborhood. "I thought no way Jello would have made it ninety-five miles," White told the newspaper.

Nevertheless, he called for Jello and was intrigued when he heard a couple of answering meows in the distance. He put a bowl of food outside, and a day later Jello showed up at his doorstep. "He was so mangy, I wasn't sure it was Jello at all," recalled White. But it was soon obvious.

"I had Jello for two years," he said. "It's undeniable. It's like having a kid. Even if he has long hair, you know he's your kid. When Jello saw it was me, he just started rubbing against my leg. He was frantic for affection and for food. All he wanted to do was eat or sit on my lap and be petted."

White said he was glad to have Jello back home. "Never underestimate the power of love," he declared.

Rusty the cat refused to accept his new digs after he and his owners moved.

For two years he navigated more than three miles of hills and busy streets to visit his former neighborhood—thirty-three times, in fact.

In 2001, when the Beidler family moved to Key West, Iowa, from Dubuque, Iowa, they kept Rusty inside to help him adjust to his new home. They thought the long-haired feline, who resembled an orange raccoon, would love their ranch house. "He had ground squirrels, birds, and field mice to chase and a nice, new house to live in," his owner, Jodi Beidler, told the *Dubuque (IA) Telegraph Herald*. "He ruled the roost around here."

No matter. One day, a few weeks after the move, Rusty broke the screen of an open front window and headed out on his first adventure.

Beidler was certain Rusty had returned to his old home. She went back to the house every day for a week, but there wasn't any sign of him. Two weeks later, she received a phone call from an old neighbor who said Rusty was sound asleep in his favorite spot on the deck of the Beidlers' former home.

Rusty was brought back to his new house, but he didn't stay long. He slipped out the kitchen door and took off for his favorite haunt. This time, it took him ten days to get there before he was spotted and picked up by his owner. Over the next two years, the cat managed to escape another thirty-one times and return to his former home. One time, he was missing for six months before he showed up in his old neighborhood.

Beidler said she didn't know why he was drawn to the old house. "I would like to strap a 'kitty-cam' to him and see where he goes and if anyone takes care of him along the way," she said.

"We usually have to give Rusty a flea bath whenever we find him and bring him home. He eats a lot and usually hangs around for a few weeks. Then he starts sniffing the air as if he's getting his bearings. When we see that, we know he's ready to leave again."

Nothing was going to stop a calico named Gribouille from living in central France—even after the cat was given to a family who moved to a town in Germany 600 miles away.

His owner, Madeleine Martinet, of Tannay, France, gave him to her neighbor, Jean-Paul Marquart, in 1987. A month later, Marquart and his family moved, taking Gribouille with them to their new home in Reutlingen, West Germany.

Apparently, Gribouille pined for his former home and owner back in France, so shortly after the move to Germany, he set out on a remarkable journey that lasted twenty-two grueling months. The determined feline trekked through forests, over mountains, around rivers, and across superhighways. He survived freezing snow, bone-chilling wind, and scorching sun.

When he finally reached Martinet's doorstep in August 1989, he was bleeding, ragged, underweight, and nearly blind from eye infections. "There's no doubt Gribouille is the same cat that left Germany," Martinet told the press. "His mother recognized him instantly. She nursed his wounds and now he's fit and well.

"This time, he's staying home for good."

A long-haired stray cat experienced a wild ride—
160 miles in the engine compartment of a car.

In December 2003, a college student drove her
Chevrolet Tracker from Kalamazoo, Michigan, to
Rochester Hills, Michigan, for the holidays. She made
the trip in three hours without stopping.

Remarkably, the cat survived just fine, emerging
from his journey unscathed. "He was very lucky,"
Patricia Verduin, board president of the Michigan
Animal Rescue League in Pontiac, told the *Daily
Oakland (MI) Press.*

The stray probably slipped into the engine compartment to keep warm shortly before the student

drove off. When the student, who declined to give her name to the league, reached home "she heard this intense kitty-crying," Verduin said. "She thought she'd run over a cat."

The woman and her family searched around the car. When they finally lifted the hood, they were shocked to find a Russian Blue Angora mixed breed sitting on top of the engine. "He was sitting very still," Verduin said. "It was like he didn't know what to do."

With a house full of pets, the woman turned the cat over to the rescue league, where he was given the name Tracker and adopted out.

Two kittens who had been catnapping on the chassis of a truck failed to jump off when it started up—and they remained clinging to their precarious perch until the vehicle reached its destination sixty miles away.

Four-month-old sisters Smokey and Dotty were black and white farm cats who lived outdoors at Hardy's Cottage Garden Plants in Whitchurch, Hampshire, England. Owner Rosy Hardy said the felines kept the nursery free from mice and other rodents.

The kittens had curled up under the nursery's delivery truck for shelter from the wind and rain on May 17, 2001. When the truck started up, they remained on the undercarriage as driver Neil Russell headed up to the Chelsea Flower Show in London. Amazingly, Smokey and Dotty spent ninety minutes perched on a tiny ledge on the truck's chassis just two feet from the ground. They didn't move a muscle, not even when the truck stopped at traffic lights or was roaring along the expressway.

Russell eventually heard meowing when he turned off the engine at his destination. As he went to open the back of the vehicle, the cats appeared at his feet. He was able to catch Smokey, who seemed in shock, but he was unable to grab Dotty, who shot off toward the flower show. Russell felt sorry for Smokey and treated her to a dinner of fish and chips.

Learning of the kittens' ordeal the next day, Hardy told the *Hampshire Chronicle* (UK), "The cats are always trying to find somewhere warm to sleep, but usually they wake up when they hear the engine."

Added Russell, "They must have held on for dear life."

Sherry the Siamese cat flew more than 225,000 miles over thirty-two days, and wasn't too thrilled about it. You couldn't blame her—she was lost in the hold of a jetliner.

In November 1979, air force sergeant Guy Jones and his wife, Ginger, shipped their two caged cats on Pan American World Airways from Guam to San Francisco to Melbourne, Florida, after he was transferred to Patrick Air Force Base. When the plane arrived, there was only one cat. Sherry's cage was unlocked and she was nowhere to be found.

"We had given up all hope on her," Sergeant Jones told the Associated Press.

But then he received word that flight personnel at London's Heathrow Airport had found Sherry in the same 747 cargo hold from which she had disappeared thirty-two days earlier. Although she was alive, Sherry was weak and starving, and her right rear leg was so badly injured it had to be amputated. It wasn't known how she had managed to survive or how she was hurt.

As soon as she recovered, the airline flew Sherry from London to Orlando, where the two-year-old cat was reunited with the Joneses.

"We figured she had unwillingly traveled 225,000 miles and touched down in twelve countries during the time she was missing," a Pan Am spokesperson said.

Ozzy the cat flew more than 63,000 miles between two continents over ten days against his wishes.

The one-year-old white-and-orange-flecked cat had been adopted by Jonathan Boyd and his partner Katie Deacon while they were working as teachers in Doha, the capital of the Persian Gulf country of Qatar. When the couple returned to their home in North Yorkshire, England, in the summer of 2002, they paid $330 to fly their pet cat back to the United Kingdom in the cargo hold of their British Airways flight.

But when they arrived in London, they were told that Ozzy was missing from his cage. Authorities suspected he had escaped while the plane was being loaded in Doha or during a stopover in Manama, the capital of Bahrain. British Airways staff searched everywhere in the plane and at the airports, and even put up posters.

"We were pretty upset about it and I got angry," Boyd told the press later. "How the hell can a cat disappear? We were told there was nowhere he could go." Boyd and Deacon were convinced that they would never see their pet again.

However, ten days later they received great news: Ozzy was found alive, although he was frightened and bewildered. Apparently, when he had escaped from his cage, he went into the rear cargo hold and hid in the tail of the plane. He remained there while the plane made its daily 6,300-mile round-trip between Qatar and London for ten days.

"When they found him, he was actually black with oil and grime on him," Boyd recalled. "He was very skinny and very nervous as well. He is a very lucky cat. He must have used up at least two of his nine lives. We are so relieved that he is safe and well."

Airport officials believe Ozzy survived by snacking on airport workers' sandwiches that they left unattended while they were loading and unloading the plane.

"We are obviously concerned that Ozzy was able to escape from his cage, but we are relieved and happy he has been reunited with his owners," a British Airways spokeswoman told the press. "He was certainly looked for thoroughly. Our team did its very best, but if a cat wants to hide, it will."

Had the cat's owners known he was going to take a great adventure, they would have signed him up for frequent flier status. The airline spokeswoman said, "If Ozzy was registered for BA Miles, he would have earned enough to travel free to Rio de Janeiro and back plus a trip or two to Europe."

A kitten hitched a ride in a private plane by hiding in the wheel well.

The tiny feline sauntered onto the tarmac in Charlotte, North Carolina, and then jumped into the wheel well of a Beech Bonanza before the single-engine plane took off.

Despite the retractable landing gear, the kitten wasn't hurt and survived the 350-mile flight to Columbus, Georgia, on May 28, 2002.

After the plane touched down in Columbus, Andy Jeffers, a line technician at CSG Aviation, began refueling the aircraft. That's when he heard what he thought was a cat's meow. "I asked the pilot if he had a cat on board," Jeffers told the *Columbus (GA) Ledger-Enquirer.* "He looked at me strangely and said, 'No.' I figured I must be hearing things." He wasn't.

Another meow convinced Jeffers to look in the wheel well. There, he found the kitten, who was only a few weeks old. The cat was shaking from fright and mewing but otherwise appeared unharmed.

The Bonanza pilot said he had no idea how the kitten was able to climb into the wheel well.

Ashley Dennard Boyett, an employee in the CSG office, called the air service in Charlotte to find out if anyone was missing a kitten. "They said they had been feeding a stray cat who recently had a litter," she recalled. "The kittens were known to sleep in the wheel wells of some of the planes."

Boyett, a cat lover, adopted the young gray feline and named him Runway. "It's amazing that Runway survived the flight," she said. "He's a great cat, our miracle cat."

He's not the first cat that she had adopted under strange circumstances. A few years earlier, Boyett was about to get into her pickup truck when she spotted a cat's tail under the front of the truck. When she went to investigate, she found a kitten that had climbed into the engine area of the truck to escape the cold. Boyett rescued the stray kitten and named him Lucky.

An Italian cat took an unexpected trip to the United States—an experience that proved to be extremely chilly and chilling.

The black cat was discovered nearly frozen to death in a huge refrigerated wine cargo container at a dock in Newark, New Jersey, on January 29, 2002. The container had been shipped across the Atlantic from a vineyard in Italy's Tuscany region three weeks earlier.

Surprised workers of Marchesi Antinori Wines found the frost-covered feline when they opened the 1,200-case shipment. They feared the worst because the green-eyed male didn't move, didn't react to a flashlight, and couldn't even be coaxed by a bowl of milk.

"Everyone thought he was dead," Francine Bryan Brown, a spokeswoman for the wine importer, told the *New York Daily News*. An animal rescue unit was called, and the cat, estimated to be about two years old, was ultimately revived and taken to Newark's Associated Humane Societies.

The workers who found the cat named him Peppoli, for the brand of Chianti that was in the container. They said the cat might have been poking around in the container in Italy just before he was accidentally locked inside. Peppoli apparently survived the three-week voyage by lapping up the condensation that had gathered along the edge of the forty-foot-long container, which was kept at 55 degrees while at sea.

Lucy the calico wanted to see the inside of a motor home— and unexpectedly ended up 2,700 miles away.

The feline was owned by Murray and Donna Arsenault, who lived in Inuvik, Northwest Terrorities, Canada. Their house was directly across the street from the town's tourist center, where many RVs stopped every day. Apparently, on July 1, 2001, Lucy walked over to the center and hopped aboard a motor home.

When Lucy failed to show up for dinner, the Arsenaults wondered what had happened to their cat. They hoped that if she were lost, someone would find her and call them because she was wearing a collar with their phone number on it.

Two weeks after she went missing, Donna received a call from a woman who said she had been looking after a stray cat.

"We got a phone call from a girl who said, 'Do you own a cat?' My wife said, 'Yes, yes, we do,'" Murray told the Canadian press. "The caller said she was in Thornhill. So my wife was trying to think where Thornhill Street was in Inuvik. She'd never heard of it."

To her stunned amazement, Donna eventually realized the woman was 2,700 miles away—in Thornhill, Ontario.

Lucy was returned home—this time by airplane.

Lapis the cat took a little walk and ended 3,000 miles from home, and in another country.

When Lapis disappeared in March 2000, her owner, Jennifer Hill, of Denver, recalled, "I cried and cried because I loved her so much." She posted signs, placed ads, and called animal shelters, but there was not a single word about the fate of her beloved cat.

None, that is, until June, seventy days later, when she received a phone call from Canada's far north—Champagne

Landing, Yukon Territory, to be exact—in a town of fifteen hardy souls who live closer to the Arctic Circle than the U.S. border.

Hill was thrilled and perplexed. How in the world did her cat end up in the Yukon? The best guess was she had hopped onto the back of a truck or camper and either leaped off or was thrown out near Champagne Landing.

Just about everyone in the former gold rush trading post had seen the five-pound feline snooping around. Edward Chambers recalled that his dog, R.V., had chased the cat up a tree. He figured the cat was abandoned or somehow came from another town but "not the other side of the Rockies."

A week later, Chambers's son-in-law, David Grant, spotted the cat pursuing field mice. He was surprised that the cat had not been killed by coyotes or wolves or other predators in the area. He also noted that the feline had a blue collar so he knew it wasn't a feral cat. Then Grant's niece coaxed the cat to come to her and checked out the tag on the collar. The phone number had an area code that she had never seen before. Grant called the number and told Hill the good news—he had her cat and Lapis was fine.

Grant drove the cat to Whitehorse, the territorial capital, bought a cage, and put her on a plane. Lapis returned home to Denver seventy days after her odyssey began and was the subject of stories around the world. Exactly what had happened to Lapis, no one will ever know. And she's not talking.

Said Hill, "When she got home, she ate a can of tuna, then played with her toys, and went to sleep."

Pip the cat jumped into an open box at his home in Connecticut and wound up accidentally sealed inside and FedExed to the Midwest.

The ordeal happened in May 2004, when his owner, Juliana Lewis, of Ledyard, Connecticut, was boxing up a wicker chair that she was returning via FedEx to a company in Missouri. Pip and some of the dozen cats that Lewis had adopted over the years watched her curiously.

"The cats decided that would be a really fun place to play and they were jumping in and out of the box," she later told reporters. Lewis thought the box was free of any felines when she sealed it. Then FedEx picked the box up from her front steps.

Because she had a dozen cats, including two black-and-white ones that looked like Pip, it wasn't until twenty-four hours later that Lewis realized Pip was missing. "All of a sudden it hit me: 'Oh my God, he's in the box!'" she recalled.

Lewis immediately called FedEx officials and told them she had accidentally sealed up the box with her cat inside. "I had a nervous day with a lot of prayers," she said.

FedEx located the box at its Indianapolis hub, where trace agent Sarfraz Khan found the cat inside, brought him to her home, and fed him. Then she took the cat to a vet to get the paperwork necessary to return him to Connecticut on a passenger flight because FedEx doesn't have a license to ship live animals.

Finally, after a three-day journey on FedEx trucks, a weekend stay with Khan, and a flight home—with a layover in Detroit—Pip was reunited with Lewis.

"He's gotten around," she said. "He's been in more states than I have."

Before leaving on a flight, British Airways purser John Pearson wanted to say good-bye to his pet Persian, Katie, but he couldn't find her. Katie usually nosed around his suitcase whenever he packed for a trip, but on this December day in 1998, she didn't respond to his calls.

Running late, Pearson didn't have time to hunt for her in the house. As he headed to the airport, he used his cell phone to leave a message for his wife at her office to make sure to look for Katie when she returned home.

Later that day, after a long flight from London to Montreal, Pearson arrived in his hotel room and opened his luggage. He jerked with surprise when, from out of the suitcase, popped his beloved cat.

Only then did he realize how Katie had become a stow-away. "While I was packing at home," Pearson later told the *Montreal Gazette*, "I was interrupted by a phone call. Unbeknownst to me, Katie jumped into my suitcase and curled up for a nap. She's mostly black and had snuggled inside my black down jacket. When I came back and finished packing, I simply didn't notice her catnapping inside.

And she didn't move. I zipped up my suitcase and called out to her to say good-bye. But if she responded, I didn't hear her."

By cuddling in Pearson's jacket and staying quiet as a mouse in the suitcase, Katie went unnoticed through security checks and in the crew's luggage compartment onboard the plane. From Pearson's London home to the Montreal hotel, Katie spent eight hours and 3,200 miles in the suitcase.

"When she sprang out of the suitcase, she was scared and ruffled, but still able to purr," said Pearson. "I was in total shock. I couldn't believe it. She didn't want to leave my sight. But she had a much better flight on the way home—she got to sit in first class."

The mystery surrounding the disappearance of Lilly the cat was an open-and-shut case. Literally.

The two-year-old Siamese disappeared on April 20, 2004, after movers showed up to pack the belongings of her owners, Henry Leonard and Vicki Plechner, of Tarrytown, New York. The couple searched everywhere for the cat, checking some of the boxes that had already been packed. They also put up reward signs around the neighborhood before leaving for their new home in Reno, Nevada.

"We were just sick," Leonard later told the *Reno Gazette-Journal*. "She was a little kitten when we got her."

In Reno, on May 5, a mover was taking the last piece of furniture off the truck when he opened a dresser drawer to get a grip on it. Surprise! There was Lilly!

She hadn't seen any of her two-week, cross-country trip because she had been in the drawer the whole time.

"We were dumbfounded, speechless," Leonard said. "You'll never find two more happy people."

Lilly appeared stunned and weak from her ordeal, but after the couple gave her water and baby food and lots of tender loving care, she was purring and running around—and staying away from dresser drawers.

A British feline had an unintended, lengthy European vacation after sleeping in the back of a moving van.

Top Cat (or T.C. for short), owned by Jayne Manley, of St. Neot, Cornwall, England, had moseyed from his house to watch a neighbor loading furniture into a van in early March 2002. Without being noticed, the ten-year-old Oriental Red then hopped inside the back of the truck and went to sleep.

"My next-door neighbor was packing a van to take some stuff to his mother who had bought property in France," Manley told the BBC. "My T.C. crawled into the back of the van. I didn't know any of this because I was away. I had a friend looking after my animals who said T.C. wasn't around."

Manley said that T.C.'s disappearance was out of character because he never strayed far from the house after being injured two years earlier in a road accident that cost him his tail and left him with bolts in his legs.

"On Monday we started looking, and we couldn't find him anywhere," she recalled. "Then on Wednesday I got a phone call saying, 'We've found your cat. He's in Bordeaux.'" That was 500 miles away.

"I just felt relief that he was alive but obviously very upset," Manley said, "and my first reaction was, 'What am I going to do?'"

T.C. didn't have a pet passport, which meant if he returned to the United Kingdom right away, he would be quarantined for seven months. That was unacceptable to Manley, so she arranged to have T.C. driven to Santander, Spain, and met him there. Then she took her peripatetic pet on a train to Malaga, where T.C. stayed with Manley's friend Heather McClerry for the necessary period of time until the cat qualified for a pet passport that would allow him to return to Cornwall.

"He had a lovely time," Manley said. "He sunbathed a lot and often joined friends on the terrace for a drink."

T.C. enjoyed seven blissful months of lapping up the sun before his pet passport was finally issued, allowing him to return to the United Kingdom. Manley was overjoyed. "It's just wonderful," she told the BBC. "I was so excited waiting for him to come home."

She said the expenses to get T.C. back home totaled about $1,500—"which would have bought a lot of cat food."

Mike the cat tried to mail himself to Europe.

A sack of mail that was destined for an overseas voyage in March 1895 was about to be transported to a ship when

A. J. Eamley, of New York City's main post office, heard a weak meow coming from the large pouch. Eamley opened the sack and was startled when a cat jumped out.

Following postal regulations, Eamley wrote an official memo to New York postmaster Dayton, stating, "I have to report that a live cat was forwarded to this office in a sack of newspapers under the accompanying label: Station W, Brooklyn." And, thus, the red tape began to unfurl.

Postmaster Dayton forwarded the memo to Superintendent Jackson of the main post office, who sent it to Postmaster Sullivan of Brooklyn, who passed it on to Superintendent Francis Morris, of Brooklyn's Station W, with this official query: "What information can be furnished by your office regarding the missending [*sic*] of this cat?"

In his official response, Superintendent Morris wrote, "This inquiry relates to our office cat, a highly prized animal. He was of an inquiring turn of mind, and happened to be in the foreign paper sack at the time of dispatch. Clerk Taylor did not know of his presence there, and tied up and forwarded the sack to your office. We will very cheerfully pay all expenses incurred by the present custodians for board, maintenance, etc., if they will return him in good condition to this office."

The response was sent to Postmaster Sullivan of Brooklyn who asked Postmaster Dayton if Station W's request could be honored. Postmaster Dayton replied in an official memo, "In accordance with the request of the Superintendent of Branch W, I have to inform you that the cat has been returned by special messenger free of all charges."

Meanwhile, Superintendent Jackson of New York made this official inquiry to Postmaster Sullivan of Brooklyn: "Has the cat come back?"

Postmaster Sullivan then forwarded the query to Superintendent Morris at Station W, who gave this official response: "The cat came back in an improved condition. Please convey to the honorable Postmaster of New York [Dayton] my most sincere thanks for the courtesy shown this office." Naturally, Postmaster Sullivan of Brooklyn forwarded Superintendent Morris's response to Superintendent Jackson of New York who then forwarded it to Postmaster Dayton.

As for Mike the cat, he stayed out of trouble by playing with all the post office's red tape.

Hero Cats

ADOPTED CATS have repaid their new families' kindness in big ways—by saving their lives.

A two-year-old fourteen-pound feline named Doc didn't get off to a good start after Bryan Rouse of Grandview, Missouri, adopted him from the Wayside Waifs Animal Shelter and Humane Society in Kansas City. Doc raced from room to room in his new home and yowled. He fought with the family's other cat, and he tried repeatedly to get into bed with Bryan's parents, Sharon and Russell, who kept shooing him off.

Late the next night, January 31, 2000, the large tomcat once again tore through the house, howling as loud as he could. Again, he jumped on Sharon and Russell while they were sleeping. They ignored him.

Next, the cat ran into the rooms of Bryan's ten-year-old niece and eleven-year-old nephew, leaped onto their chests, and woke them up. Then he scampered down to the basement where Bryan was sleeping and woke him up too. "He was meowing so loudly I knew something was wrong," Bryan told *Cats* magazine. "When I opened the door at the top of the stairs, I saw a bright orange glow from the kitchen."

Meanwhile, Doc dashed back upstairs and jumped on Sharon and Russell until they finally were awakened and smelled smoke.

Just then the smoke detectors began blaring. Bryan yelled, "Fire! Get out of the house!" Everyone, including Doc and the other cat, fled the burning house. Bryan, a firefighter for twelve years, managed to put out the fire with a hose.

When the fire department arrived, inspectors discovered that an electrical surge had damaged a light, which sparked and ignited the curtains. "Firefighters are called heroes all the time, but we're just doing our jobs," Bryan said. "Doc is a real hero. He acted quicker than the smoke detectors."

Doc's selfless act of courage earned the once orphaned feline the June Lewyt Award, given by the North Shore Animal League America, an organization based in Port Washington, New York, that gives out a monthly award to a deserving pet.

In a similar case, a pet cat warned his adoptive family of a fire.

Jon and Kimberly Reiman of Salt Lake City had rescued a stray cat's newborn kittens after they became trapped behind a wall of a backyard shed in 1994. When the mama cat refused to take her babies back, the Reiman family bottle-fed the kittens until they were old enough to be adopted. Although they already had two cats, the Reimans kept one of the kittens and named him Brother.

He proved to be more than just a loving, delightful cat. He proved to be a lifesaver.

What he did on the night of April 5, 1999, earned him the June Lewyt Award, just like Doc. Here's what happened, according to award judge Kristin von Kreisler:

> That evening, Kimberly turned on the dishwasher and got ready for bed. Pacing around the kitchen, the loyal feline kept meowing and meowing at Kimberly.

She thought he wanted food, but she found his bowl full, so she opened the front door to see if he wanted out. He didn't. He just sat there in the kitchen looking frantic and distressed. "I thought he was just being silly," recalls Kimberly. So, she went to her bedroom and closed the door.

Brother did not give up. Instead, he went downstairs to the bedroom where the Reiman daughters were also settling down for the night. He pushed open the door and leaped on Chelsea's bed and pressed relentlessly on the teenager's arm. "Go away, Brother," mumbled Chelsea, slightly annoyed, as she continued to read her book. But the persistent cat would not give up. He meowed again and clawed her leg as if to say, "Listen! This is *really* urgent!"

Assuming he just wanted out, Chelsea started up the stairs to the front door. Suddenly, she smelled smoke.

She peeked into the kitchen and saw that the dishwasher was engulfed in flames. The new smoke alarms had not yet been installed, so no alarms were working in the house that night.

"Without Brother, it could have been really tragic," Kimberly said. "We could easily have died from smoke inhalation." It may have taken Brother five years, but he certainly repaid the Reimans for rescuing him from the storage shed.

A year after he had been rescued from an animal shelter, a brown domestic shorthair named Ito became a hero.

One day in 1997, his owner, Johanna Tanner of Lompoc, California, had removed her glasses and was getting ready to take a shower when she heard a thumping noise in the family room. She went to investigate, but without her glasses it was hard to see, although she could tell that Ito was beside the sliding glass door.

Johanna began to move in for a closer look when she heard a strange rattling sound. As she stepped forward, Ito rammed into her ankles. Barefoot, Johanna continued on until Ito blocked her path. By now she could clearly see that a rattlesnake had somehow entered the house.

The cat then attacked the snake, but the reptile struck back and bit the brave feline on the right front paw. Although the rattler was coiled and hissing and ready for another strike, Johanna scooped up Ito and yelled for her husband, Roger, who then killed the snake.

Meanwhile, Johanna placed Ito on the dining room table, grasped his injured paw above the puncture marks, and expressed some of the venom from the wound. After wrapping the cat in a towel with an ice compress on the injury and maintaining pressure above the wound, the couple rushed Ito to the animal hospital where he was treated and sent home to convalesce for a week.

"I just can't help thinking what would have happened if Ito hadn't seen the snake," Johanna told *Cats* magazine. "That thing could have settled under a bed and bitten one of us in the morning or gotten one of the other pets."

Fully recovered, Ito—named after a certain judge in a notorious murder trial—was soon back to his old self. "The only change we've noticed is an intense snake fetish," Johanna said. Anything even resembling a snake— pantyhose, bathrobe belts, a vacuum hose, or a garden hose—was worthy of a preemptive attack.

When an intruder sneaked into her owner's house, a sweet calico named Aggie launched into a ferocious attack that drove him away. What made her heroics so remarkable was that Aggie was blind.

"It was frightening to have a burglar enter our home while we were sound asleep," said Lynn Seely, of Falling Waters, West Virginia. "He would have robbed us if it hadn't been for Aggie's brave actions. How she knew to attack him is a mystery. She had never scratched a person in her life except for that incident."

When Lynn and her husband, John, lived in Mechanicsburg, Pennsylvania, in 1989, they adopted a sick, blind, orphaned kitten and named her Aggie. After being nursed back to health, Aggie grew into a smart, lovable cat who learned to function just fine despite her disability. She displayed a delightful, gentle nature. No one knew she had the heart and courage of a lion.

During the winter of 1992, a burglar had been breaking into area homes in the wee hours of the morning. One night at about three a.m., Aggie was curled up on the bed of her sleeping owners when she was wakened by an unusual noise. She crept downstairs and climbed onto her seven-foot-tall cat tree located next to a window that the intruder had pried open. The burglar looked inside but never noticed the large calico perched on her cat tree.

"Aggie had been listening intently to the faint sounds of the screen being removed and the window being opened," said Lynn, who agreed to share her story. "She knew something wasn't quite right. She didn't like the suspicious way the window was opened, she didn't like the cold air pouring in, and she especially didn't like the smell of this strange menacing person who was standing just outside of her window."

The robber stood on two stacked cinder blocks, gripped both sides of the window frame, and quietly eased himself through. Meanwhile, Aggie's ears were straining to catch any sound. She waited until she sensed he was right next to her.

"As he took the next step, Aggie attacked," Lynn said. "She leaped onto his face, scratched deeply, and then jumped to safety. The panicked prowler screamed in terror and stumbled backward out of the window.

"The bloodcurdling scream woke us and we bolted upright in bed, hearts racing. Once downstairs, we saw the window was wide open and, oddly, a shoe was balanced on the windowsill. There were a couple of snowy footprints in the room by the cat tree. It was then I noticed Aggie. All her fur stood out and made her look twice her normal size. She was facing me, her tail swishing back and forth, and seemed really proud of herself. Her white paws and white chin had blood on them, but when I examined Aggie carefully she wasn't hurt. Then I noticed blood on the windowsill. It became very clear to me what had happened—Aggie had attacked the intruder.

"A police officer arrived a few minutes later and surveyed the scene. He discovered the intruder had left behind a few tools and odd footprints in the snow leading away from the window—one sock print and one shoe print.

"The officer said a number of robberies had taken place in the area and that this robber preferred homes that didn't have a dog. Then he added with a grin that the robber would probably think twice about invading a home with a cat, too."

About a month later, police arrested a suspect and charged him with several neighborhood burglaries. "Although the suspect wasn't charged with breaking into our home, he did have deep scratches on his face," Lynn said. "We're convinced he was the one who Aggie attacked."

Spikester the cat saved the life of his teenage owner when she suffered a diabetic seizure.

On the morning of June 17, 2004, Bob Smithee was drinking coffee and watching the news on television in the bedroom of his home in Medford, Oregon, when Spikester, the family's three-year-old orange tabby, entered his room, acting strangely.

"He came and jumped on my bed, stretching and looking down the hallway and acting all weird," Smithee told the *Medford (OR) Mail Tribune*. "He meowed and turned away and ran down the hallway" to the bedroom door of Smithee's fifteen-year-old daughter, Christina.

Smithee got up and followed Spikester, who scratched at Christina's door. When Smithee opened it, he found his daughter semiconscious in the throes of a seizure.

Christina, an insulin-dependent Type 1 diabetic, had experienced a drop in blood sugar, which caused her first-ever seizure as she slept. Paramedics were called and they rushed Christina to the emergency room at Rogue Valley Medical Center, where she made a quick recovery.

"If the cat hadn't let me know, you can only think what would have happened," Smithee told the paper.

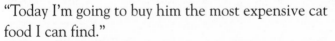

"Today I'm going to buy him the most expensive cat food I can find."

A spokesperson for the Delta Society, a national organization that promotes service animals, said that certain gifted pets, mostly dogs, have been known to warn people about approaching seizures. The animals are either born with the ability to sense seizures or not, said Michelle Cobey of the Delta Society. "Some think it's an odor, some people think it's something else," she said. "The truth is, nobody really knows."

Christina, who's convinced that Spikester saved her life, said, "It's like something you'd see in a movie that wouldn't really happen, but it did."

A pet cat thwarted the abduction of a little girl.

A seven-year-old girl was holding her cat while walking in her neighborhood in Lansing, Michigan, on March 27, 2002, when a man snatched her from his front lawn, according to police.

The abductor brought the girl and her cat inside his home while she screamed and yelled at him to let her go, Lieutenant Steve Mitchell told the *Lansing (MI) State Journal*. Investigators say the man tried to put tape over the child's mouth after she told him she heard her mother calling for her. Then he tried to take off her pants but couldn't, said Detective Brian Smitherman.

Realizing that the little girl was in increasing danger, the cat, which the girl had been holding the entire time, sprang into action. He swiped at the abductor's arm, sinking his claws deep into the man's skin. The abductor shouted in pain, enabling the girl to break free and escape. Still clutching her cat, the girl ran home and reported the crime.

The Lansing police special tactical team went to the alleged abductor's home with a search warrant, and found him hiding in a crawl space in the basement, covered in dirt to conceal himself, Lieutenant Mitchell said.

Police arrested Wulfrido Lopez, thirty-six, who was arraigned on a charge of kidnapping and child enticement, which is punishable by up to life in prison. He also was charged with criminal sexual conduct. He was jailed on $300,000 bond.

"She was damn lucky she had that cat in her hand," Detective Smitherman said. "Otherwise this could have turned out really bad."

Tiger the cat proved that he was aptly named.

With the fury of his namesake, Tiger fought off an intruder who was attacking the cat's defenseless mistress. The feline's heroism came to light in a letter to the editor in the *New York Times*. It was written on April 11, 1899, by H. I. Watts. Here is what he wrote:

> I have a cat, Tiger by name, which is one of the gentlest creatures I have ever seen, so kind and affectionate. No matter how many homeless tabbies come around, he always has a smile of welcome for them.
>
> One night last month, my wife was alone in the house and, hearing a knock at the basement door, went downstairs and opened it when she beheld a drunken tramp. Without a word, he thrust his leg [between the door and the doorjamb], and in reply to a question as to what he wanted, he replied, "Money to get a night's lodging and something to eat."

"Remove your foot and I will get you what you want," she said, terrified almost to fainting.

"No, ha, ha!" he said, and then, suspecting she was alone, thrust his foot further and soon had her pressed against the wall [until she was] almost breathless and on the point of fainting.

She felt something whiz past her shoulder, and a yell of pain came from the tramp. "Oh, what's that?" he cried.

Tiger had been asleep in the kitchen and, hearing the commotion, darted [from the stairs] over my wife's shoulder and into the brute's face.

With a rush for the street where he went sprawling, what might have been a tragedy ended safely, and dear old Tiger had saved his mistress's life.

A frail calico named Patches helped save her owner from serious injury and possibly death—by using what arguably could be called extrasensory feline perception.

"For as long as I remember, I've believed animals knew things we didn't, but it took Patches to prove it to me," said Alice Thompson of Baltimore, who agreed to share her story.

On the night of March 17, 1995, Alice had returned home from a party when she spotted Patches outside her kitchen. The cat, owned by neighbors Mike and Sandy (who did not want their last names used), often paid her a visit because Alice liked to give Patches a treat.

But on this particular night, Patches ignored the tasty can of Whiskas. Acting uncharacteristically skittish and agitated, she jumped from the backyard wall to the air-conditioning unit to the ground by Alice's shoes to the gardening cart and then to the top of a gate. Not grabbing Alice's attention, the cat repeated the sequence.

Figuring it was nothing more than the night crazies, Alice went back inside the house to watch TV. Shortly after midnight, she returned to the kitchen and noticed Patches staring at her from the other side of the glass terrace doors, mewing away. Thinking something in the alley was frightening her, Alice went outside and looked up and down the alley, but saw nothing unusual.

Patches, however, ran down the alley, stopping every few seconds to look back at Alice, who presumed the cat was beckoning her. Seeing Alice follow her, the cat ran home and stood with her front paws on the door. Then she started mewing as though she wanted to be let in. Alice recalled, "I explained to her it was close to 12:30 a.m., and I couldn't knock on the door at that time of night, but she showed no sense of understanding and continued her cries for assistance."

Alice finally knocked on the door until a very drowsy Mike answered it. "I apologized and explained his cat's bizarre behavior," she recalled. "He didn't seem to mind my intrusion. He simply opened the door for Patches and said he had to get up anyway. He apparently had fallen asleep on the sofa. I then returned home. End of story, or so I thought."

The next morning, while walking her dog Magoo, Alice bumped into Sandy. "She seemed rather excited and said, 'Thank you so much for waking up Michael last night.' Perplexed with this statement, I just smiled and began talking about Patches's peculiar behavior the evening before," Alice said.

They strolled down the sidewalk until they were in front of Sandy's house. "I noticed the entire bay window had been broken," Alice recalled. "'My God,' I exclaimed, 'what happened?'

"Sandy explained that the broken window was the reason for her thanking me. Mike had been sleeping on the sofa immediately below the window prior to my waking him up. Ten minutes later, a gunshot had come through that same window. Glass shards had covered and perforated the entire sofa. She said if Mike had still been sleeping there, he would have suffered serious injuries. More likely, she said swallowing hard, he would have been killed."

The potentially deadly drive-by shooting was never solved, but thanks to Patches, no one was hurt.

Puss Puss, a black-and-white house cat, helped save the life of a drowning lamb.

The cat, who was somewhat disabled, had accompanied her owners while they worked on a private garden in Icomb, Gloucestershire, England, on October 5, 2003. Puss Puss was lounging by the pool when a lamb escaped from a small flock of sheep that was grazing in a nearby field. Somehow the lamb tumbled into the pool and was thrashing about.

Behaving like the dog Lassie during times of trouble, the cat frantically meowed and ran back and forth between the pool and the garden, trying to alert her owners of an emergency.

Her owners, gardeners Adrian Bunton and Karen Lewis, knew something was wrong when they saw their cat meowing and trying to communicate with them.

Jill Royle, whose garden they were working in, said, "She was in a very, very agitated state, meowing and calling and crying and being an utter pest and dashing back and forward between them and the pool."

The cat's owners finally followed her back to the pool and found the drowning lamb under the pool cover with his head entangled in the cover's straps. Bunton jumped into the pool and pulled out the lamb. The animal was scared but otherwise OK and was returned to the flock.

Praising her lifesaving cat, Lewis told the *Gloucestershire Echo* (UK), "She's a real little superstar."

The actions of the quick-thinking feline are all the more remarkable because Puss Puss was partially handicapped. "As a kitten she had an accident and had to have her tail amputated," Lewis told the Animal News Center. "She hasn't grown properly, has arthritis, and can't curl up, jump, or climb like other normal cats."

Royle wrote about the incident in the village newsletter, telling readers, "If you see a little black cat with no tail walking in Icomb, it will be gallant Puss Puss, who deserves a medal."

Mews Items

Fritz the cat saved his mother from an accidental hanging.

Born in a one-kitten litter in 1984, Fritz—named after Democratic presidential candidate Walter "Fritz" Mondale—was very close to his mother, Nena, owned by author Beatriz Salcedo-Strumpf of Manlius, New York. Fritz had formed such a bond with his mother that he nursed from Nena for a year.

Fritz proved to be the smartest in a house of seven cats. He was even seen urinating in the toilet and trying to flush with his paw. But his greatest achievement was helping save his mother's life.

"Fritz woke me up in the middle of the night with very loud meows," Salcedo-Strumpf told the *Syracuse (NY) Post-Standard* in 2000. "At first I thought he was hungry and offered him some food. To my surprise, he rejected it. Instead he insisted that I follow him to the closet. Suddenly I saw his mother, Nena, hanging from one of the hangers by her collar. She almost asphyxiated." Apparently, Nena became snagged while exploring a shelf in the closet.

"Somehow, Fritz knew she was dying and that I was the only one who could save her."

Rueben the cat showed he wasn't afraid of dogs—no matter how vicious. In fact, he came to the rescue of two Chihuahuas who were being attacked by two pit bulls.

Jane Hatch of Salt Lake City was walking her two Chihuahuas down the street on May 26, 2004. "The next thing I knew, both pit bulls were out and each had grabbed a dog, and I just started screaming," she told reporters.

Hearing the commotion, neighbor Stephanie Buchta came to Hatch's aid. "I was sitting on the couch and I heard screaming, I mean, bloodcurdling screaming," Buchta recalled.

Hatch said, "I tried to get them off. I kicked them, but they would not let go. I just felt so helpless."

The pit bulls were biting deep into the Chihuahuas. That's when the courageous cat jumped into the fray. "Rueben came running down and he jumped onto one of the pit bulls," recalled Hatch. While Reuben was on the dog's back, he sank his claws into its side. The dog yelped and stopped its attack. The cat's assault also distracted the other pit bull, allowing the women to snatch up the bleeding Chihuahuas.

"I put my hand on her chest to try to stop the bleeding," Buchta said of the most seriously injured Chihuahua. The tiny dogs managed to survive their injuries, although one was left with massive scars. Animal control officers put the two pit bulls under house arrest.

Praising Rueben, Buchta said, "It's not every day a cat takes on a pit bull—two of them, no less."

A neighborhood feline known as Timmy the tomcat alerted the owners of a family cat that their pet was trapped in a shed.

One night in September 2003 in the town of Blaenau Ffestiniog, Wales, Timmy, a well-known stray in the area, was using his paws to hit the back door of Duncan Hucker's house. When Hucker's son went to investigate, the cat ran into the road and waited.

"Seeing this as unusual, we all followed him down the road to the edge of the fields where we thought we could hear our own cat Meep crying," Hucker wrote in Moggycat's Cat Page, a Web site devoted to felines. "My wife and son then proceeded to check out the fields in case she had been caught up in a snare. I saw the tomcat 'dancing' along a gateway and making some very strange noises. I stopped to watch him and he ran off into a garden. The next thing I knew he was on top of an outbuilding, tapping the front with his paw.

"I called everyone over, and my son (who has the best hearing) thought he could hear a cat crying in the shed. By this time I thought I was in a Disney movie, but we called on the shed's owner and asked her to check the situation out. As soon as the door was open, a very bedraggled cat [Hucker's pet Meep] ran out and came straight to us! At this point the tom ran off, obviously happy to have sorted things out."

Leoloe the tomcat saved the lives of two children
by attacking a cobra that was ready to strike them.

The white and ginger feline was lying in the
shade of a tree outside the house of his owners,
Mr. and Mrs. Boetie Grassman, in Westering,
South Africa, on the afternoon of October 16,
1967. Leoloe was watching the Grassmans' children, Frederick, six, and Jennifer, four, playing
in the garden.

Suddenly, a five-foot-long cobra slithered
between the children. Jennifer tried to kill the
snake by stomping on its tail, but the cobra reared
for attack.

Seeing the danger, Leoloe leaped up and
charged the snake. The cat swiftly pounced on

the cobra, biting it behind its hood. The children sprinted into the house to call their father. Meanwhile, the cat kept the snake at bay until Grassman came out and killed it with a stick.

The excitement over, Leoloe trotted back to the shade tree and calmly went to sleep.

For his quick action and bravery, the cat was awarded a medal for valor by the Eastern Province Cat Club at its championship show in Port Elizabeth, South Africa.

Buster the prison cat foiled the escape of a notorious murderer.

Jesse Pomeroy was serving a life sentence of solitary confinement at Charlestown State Prison in Massachusetts for the torture and slaying of two children. He had been incarcerated for thirty-six years—ever since he was convicted as a teenager—when he tried to break out on December 30, 1912.

About 2:30 a.m., guard Thomas Brassil was patrolling the solitary confinement wing. He passed Buster, the warden's yellow cat and prison mascot, who was curled up asleep on a wooden chair in the hall. All of a sudden, Buster, his tail and hair bristling, let out a yowl and raced past him.

The guard drew his gun, turned around, and retraced his steps until he saw Buster meowing at something. Then Brassil spotted a prisoner crouched in the shadows and the guard ordered the inmate to get to his feet. In the light he could see it was Pomeroy, who was holding a large screwdriver in his right hand. After a brief scuffle, the guard locked the killer into a secure cell.

Pomeroy confessed that he had obtained an improvised saw and had spent three years sawing through the bars at the bottom of his steel cell door. He stuffed his blanket with an old carton and a bunch of newspapers to make it appear he was sleeping. Then he squeezed out of the sawed-off bars and opened an outer wooden door by sticking his arm through the food slot and using the saw to work the iron bolt from its socket. He made it to the hallway and planned to short out the electric box, throwing the solitary confinement wing into darkness so he could escape in the confusion.

Everything was going according to plan—but he hadn't counted on Buster. Just as Pomeroy reached the electric box, the cat began following him and meowing, which alerted the guard.

Buster became a local hero and gained fame as the prison cat who caught the biggest rat of all—killer Jesse Pomeroy.

A police cat named Rusik was so successful in Russia's campaign against the cutthroat and lucrative world of caviar smuggling that he was targeted for assassination.

Rusik displayed an amazing ability to sniff out poached fish hidden in trucks and other vehicles. He was then recruited by police at a checkpoint in the Stavropol region, which borders the Caspian Sea, to find illegal cargoes of endangered sturgeon and quickly became the scourge of the coast's caviar mafia.

Mews Items

The area had been plagued by poachers determined to cash in on stolen sturgeon—whose roe is the delicacy caviar—which sell for huge sums in Moscow and other cities. Powerful criminal groups control a caviar black market estimated at $1.6 billion a year. Almost 95 percent of the world's caviar comes from the Caspian Sea, and because this market is so profitable, sturgeon have been hunted to the brink of extinction.

Rusik became a crime fighter by accident. He was a stray Siamese kitten in 2002 when he wandered into the police checkpoint in Stavropol and captured their hearts. They adopted him, named him Rusik, and fed him scraps of fish confiscated from smugglers. They figured he would make a cute mascot and had no idea just how special he was.

"One day Rusik just leaped into the trunk of a passing car at the checkpoint and immediately sniffed out some sturgeon," police officer Sergei Kovalenko told reporters. "After that, we decided to use him all the time."

The little cat proved to be a formidable detective. No matter how ingenious the smugglers were in their attempts to hide the fish in their vehicles, Rusik always was able to point his nose in the right direction. His sniffing skills reportedly led to the arrest of several smugglers and he consistently outperformed dogs that worked at other checkpoints.

Russia's crime-busting feline did his job too well. On July 14, 2003, Russian Ren television reported that Rusik had been run over and killed in what police believe was a contract murder. The cat was hit by a car in which he had found smuggled sturgeon months earlier, the station reported. He died under the wheels of the vehicle, which moved as he was about to detect some hidden salmon, the RIA Novosti news agency reported. Police at the checkpoint where Rusik worked said the driver appeared to have moved the car deliberately.

Rusik was killed only days after he came to the attention of the international media, which had filed glowing stories about the feline. According to RIA Novosti, police said that they were deeply saddened by Rusik's murder, but stressed that he had set a valuable precedent. They planned to train other cats to follow in his footsteps.

However, the caviar mafia isn't ready to give up, and apparently is willing to stoop to any measure to battle the feline sleuths. Rusik's pal, another fish-sniffing cat named Barsik—which means little snow leopard—died a few weeks earlier after eating a poisoned mouse.

A feline soldier who saw combat in Iraq was given a promotion and sent to the United States to live out his life in peace.

The tiger-striped cat, an Egyptian Mau, was born to a stray at a U.S. base in Balad, Iraq, fifty miles north of Baghdad. He quickly pawed his way into the hearts of the troops of the U.S. Army's 3rd Brigade Combat Team, who dubbed him Private Hammer, after the name of their unit, Team Hammer.

"He went through mortar attacks," Staff Segeant Rick Bousfield told the American Forces Press Service. "He'd jump and get scared like the rest of us. He was kind of like one of our own." Whenever the unit was attacked by mortar fire, Hammer would run to the bunkers, where the nearest soldier would scoop him up and put him inside his body armor for safekeeping.

Hammer had the run of the base and carried out his main duty—mouse patrol—like a professional. "He kept the mice out of the mess hall and living quarters," Bousfield told the *Colorado Springs Gazette*. Like his comrades, Hammer had to earn his rank. He was promoted to private first class after nabbing five mice. "He should have been a major," Bousfield said. "He caught a rat as big as he was."

The cat also chased away the blues, providing warmth and companionship in an otherwise hostile environment. Often when a soldier was wounded, the cat was brought to the hospital to cheer him up.

"He was like our stress therapist over there," recalled Bousfield, a nineteen-year army veteran. "We'd come in off raids where we'd been kicking in doors and guys would be sitting outside by themselves. They were tired and stressed. He'd come over and take their minds off the war. He wiped away some of the worries."

In January 2004, when Bousfield learned that his unit would be leaving Iraq in March to return to their home base in Fort Carson, Colorado, he knew he couldn't leave Hammer behind. So he sent an e-mail asking for help to Alley Cat Allies, a national nonprofit clearinghouse for information on feral and stray cats. The sergeant said he wanted to ensure his whole unit came home together, and that included Hammer.

The cat "has been quite a morale booster for us, because we consider him one of our troops," Bousfield wrote. "If there is a way that ACA could help get Hammer back to the States, it would be a wonderful boost for the men to see the cat, who has won their hearts, free—like the Iraqi people."

Recalled ACA national director Becky Robinson, "This was a soldier in Iraq writing to us. How could we say no to a soldier in Iraq fighting for freedom?"

ACA went on a mission to save Private Hammer. The organization joined forces with Military Mascots, a grass-roots all-volunteer group that helps deployed service members who have befriended a pet on foreign soil. Supporters' donations, combined with money from ACA's Compassion Fund, paid for Hammer's medical and travel expenses, which totaled $2,500. Working with a veterinary hospital in Kuwait that neutered the cat and gave him a clean bill of health, they arranged an international flight for Hammer to the United States.

Meanwhile Bousfield and his unit returned home from Iraq in early April 2004. Days later, Hammer flew from Kuwait to San Francisco in cargo class. Then he traveled first class with an ACA volunteer to Denver, where he was reunited with Bousfield. The ACA volunteer said the cat started purring and kneading her arm as soon as he heard Bousfield's voice. The wartime bond that had formed thousands of miles away had not been forgotten.

Back at Fort Carson, Hammer became reacquainted with his former army buddies. "They were happy to see him," Bousfield said.

Hammer then moved into his new home in a Colorado Springs subdivision with Bousfield's family, which included a wife, two teens, five cats (all former strays), a dog, two hamsters, and two geckos. Bousfield said, "They all get along now that they've gotten the pecking order straight."

No cat defined feline bravery in World War II more than a tabby named Faith.

As a two-year-old stray, she walked into St. Augustine and St. Faith's Church in London in 1936 and was adopted by Father Henry Ross, the rector. He gave her the title of official church cat and christened her Faith.

Mews Items

The tabby, who lived in the rectory adjoining the church, became a favorite of parishioners. She often sat in the first pew during Mass or sometimes lay at Father Ross's feet while he delivered his sermon. She kept the church free of mice and enjoyed being spoiled by the church ladies.

In August 1940, Faith gave birth to a black-and-white tom Father Ross called Panda. In honor of the birth, the boys' choir sang "All Things Bright and Beautiful" at Sunday Mass. Faith nursed Panda in a comfy basket in a top-floor room of the four-story rectory. But in early September, Faith became restless and agitated. She went from room to room as though looking for something. Eventually, Faith took her kitten out of the basket and carried him by the scruff of the neck to the dark, damp, cold basement.

When Father Ross discovered the basket was empty, he searched for the cats and found them in a basement corner between a pile of musty music sheets and dusty old books. He brought the cats back upstairs. Moments later, Faith seized Panda and carried him downstairs again. Father Ross took them back upstairs. This battle of the wills was repeated four times before the rector gave up and brought their basket down to the basement for them to curl up in.

Three nights later, on September 9, the Nazis launched another massive blitz on London that killed hundreds of people and destroyed dozens of buildings, including part of St. Augustine and St. Faith's Church and the rectory. When Father Ross, who had been hiding in an air raid shelter, returned to the scene, he was devastated to see the rectory in flaming ruins.

Nevertheless, he started searching for Faith and Panda even though firefighters said it was hopeless. As he picked his way through the smoking rubble, he called out to Faith several times, never expecting an answer. But then he heard a faint meow from under a pile of timber and concrete.

Peering down, he saw the brave little cat in a basement corner hemmed in by charred books and sheet music. She appeared serene and unafraid, and had her kitten between her paws. With tears of relief streaming down his face, Father Ross hacked a passage through the debris and then coaxed Faith and Panda to come out. Both were covered in grime but unhurt.

They were taken to the church vestry minutes before the rest of the bombed-out rectory collapsed in ruins. Faith stayed in the vestry and calmly settled down with Panda, knowing they were safe.

When Mass resumed at the church, Father Ross put up a picture of Faith on the chapel wall with the following typed inscription: "Faith: our dear little church cat of St. Augustine and St. Faith. The *bravest* cat in the world.

On Monday, September 9, 1940, she endured horrors and perils beyond the power of words to tell. Shielding her kitten in a sort of recess in the house (a spot she selected three days before the tragedy occurred), she sat the whole frightful night of bombing and fire, guarding her little kitten. The roofs and masonry exploded. The whole house blazed. Four floors fell through in front of her. Fire and water and ruin all around her. Yet she stayed calm and steadfast and waited for help. We rescued her in the early morning while the place was still burning, and by the mercy of Almighty God, she and her kitten were not only saved, but unhurt. God be praised and thanked for His goodness and mercy to our dear little pet."

Faith's courage inspired a nation. In a ceremony during which she sat in the lap of the Archbishop of Canterbury, the cat received a special silver medal "for steadfast courage in the Battle of London" from England's most respected animal league. Word of Faith's bravery spread around the world, and the Greenwich Village Humane League of New York presented her with a prestigious certificate of honor.

While Panda eventually became the revered residential cat of a London nursing home, Faith continued her duties as the church cat. She died in her sleep at age fourteen on September 28, 1948, and was buried on the church grounds. Her legacy lives on as the feline heroine of World War II.